'Tony and Frances' book is approachable, highly readable and great fun. It integrates the Christian message with everyday stories and shows that faith is about normal life. Great reading!'

Rev. Dr Rob Frost, evangelist, author and broadcaster.

'When Jesus said, 'Let the children come to me,' he was doing more than creating space to spend some time with a small group of curious kids. He was stating a spiritual principle that we need to be childlike in our approach to him. *Like A Child* captures the essence of this truth and in a series of short, funny, poignant stories leads us closer to the heart of the gospel. The purity and simplicity expressed in these pages is both charming and captivating.'

Peter Kerridge, Managing Director of Premier Christian Radio.

70 Thoughts for Busy Grown-ups

Like a Child

**For daily quiet times
and a resource for speakers
and teachers**

TONY AND FRANCES MILES

God bless,

Tony Miles

ROOFTOPS PUBLISHING
Loughton

First published 2003 by Rooftops Publishing
260 High Road, Loughton, Essex, IG10 1RB.

ISBN 0 9544038 0 0

Book design and production for the publisher by
Bookprint Creative Services, P.O. Box 827, BN21 3YJ, England.
Printed in Great Britain.

For Hannah and Jonathan
and in loving memory of Grandma Pat

*'Train a child in the way he should go,
and when he is old he will not turn from it.'*

Proverbs 22:6

Contents

Foreword by Diane Louise Jordan

I first met Tony Miles a few years ago on a warm spring Saturday morning, when his light airy tones brightened our family breakfast table. A welcome guest with an easy manner, he talked effortlessly, revealing his passion for God and love of people. I liked him instantly, and that Saturday morning was the first of many regular encounters with this lovely man. Of course our friendship was totally one-sided at this stage. I was just one of the many loyal fans and regular listeners to his Saturday morning show on Premier Radio – a show that has reassurance and acceptance stamped all over it.

Now, to my delight, the heart of 'Miles in the Morning' has been masterfully mirrored in this beautiful book. And what a real family affair! Written by Tony and his wonderful wife Frances but, crucially, inspired by Hannah and Jonathan. The Miles family has the gift of communicating the gospel in a down to earth 'graspable' way!

Using simple, domestic situations, together with Bible references to illuminate great teachings, *Like A Child* is an excellent resource for daily prayers and meditation. These insightful, heart-warming stories remind us, not only how precious our children are, and how much we can learn from *all* our everyday circumstances, but most importantly that God is *always* in every situation.

Warmly written, this is a quietly challenging book. I was repeatedly encouraged to look at myself, my family life, and my walk with God – yet never once did I feel condemned. The pages of *Like A Child* flow with grace and humility – a tribute to the great guy whom I finally had the privilege of meeting face to face, and his amazing family.

I highly recommend this book to everyone!

Diane Louise Jordan, television presenter, corporate speaker, vice-president of NCH, a trustee of BBC's Children in Need, and patron of many other charities.

Authors' Preface

The aim of this book is to raise a smile and inspire your thinking. We decided to write down some of the things our children said and did, not to show them up to be ignorant or misguided, but that we might learn from them. By keeping a little notebook we preserved some of those special moments that can bring great joy and which could otherwise have been lost forever. It has never been our intention to embarrass Hannah and Jonathan in any way – we have learnt and laughed together! We were (and still are) humbled by the honesty and simplicity of their words and actions. It's as we have talked about these treasured moments at the end of the day that we've been able to reflect before God. We are proud of our daughter and son and hope that when they are older, they'll find God speaking to them as they read this book, just as he has spoken to us. Frequently we've been moved and challenged by the purity of their faith or the transparency of their thinking. By being receptive to God's Spirit in all this, we believe that they have taught us so much. Apart from our Lord, of course, none of the people referred to within these pages are perfect – far from it! We trust that you will accept that these thoughts arise from a normal family life – well, as normal as living in a Methodist manse can be!

Each thought was initially written for broadcast on Premier Christian Radio by Tony as a part of the *M&M Show* on Saturday mornings, and latterly *Miles in the Morning*. We are very grateful to listeners who have written, emailed and phoned to say how much they have appreciated us sharing these reflections. The original scripts included the ages of Hannah and Jonathan at the time in the actual text, but to avoid repetition we've printed this information above each reflection. We have added suggested Bible readings and our own prayers to aid devotion.

We are indebted to those who have been a source of practical help and encouragement: thanks to Chris and Keith Watts, and John Robins for reading the text and making constructive suggestions. We are grateful to Mary Hobbs for making time to proofread the final manuscript. Rob Frost and Peter Kerridge have also been very supportive. It was Peter who encouraged Tony to record these thoughts and also gave him the opportunity to broadcast on a regular basis – first at Ten 17 (Harlow) and then at Premier. Moreover, our lips are full of nothing but *songs of praise* for Diane Louise Jordan. Thank you, Diane, for all that you do and for writing such a generous foreword. *And finally* . . . thank you Hannah and Jonathan for everything!

It's our hope that by reading this book, it will encourage you to take more time to listen to the children around you and so catch a glimpse of the kingdom of God.

Tony and Frances, January 2003.

'Wisdom is oftentimes nearer when we stoop than when we soar.' *William Wordsworth (1770–1850)*

Introduction: Biblical Basis

Jesus said: *'Let the little children come to me, and do not hinder them, for the kingdom of God belongs to such as these. I tell you the truth, anyone who will not receive the kingdom of God like a little child will never enter it.' (Mark 10:14b–15)*

People tried to bring children to Jesus but the disciples intervened. It may have been that Jewish mothers were enthusiastically bringing their little ones for a blessing. Apparently, this was something that was sought from eminent Rabbis, particularly when a child had reached his or her first birthday. Yet, the disciples thought they knew best. After all, they'd spent a lot of time alone with their Lord, discussing his teaching and asking questions. They were Jesus' special friends and he was no doubt weary from his speaking and surely didn't want to be disturbed by noisy, excitable, clingy children. How wrong they were! We fancy that Jesus was the sort of person who drew infants to him like a magnet. Though we should note that in Isaiah 53 it says:

'. . . He had no beauty or majesty to attract us to him, nothing in his appearance that we should desire him.' (Isaiah 53:2)

Perhaps this was true of adults, but what of children? We're sure you've met unassuming people who have a wonderful way with youngsters and attract them without effort or expressed desire. This is what we imagine Jesus to be like.

Could it be that he even drew strength from the children drawn to his side?

Earlier in Mark's Gospel *(9:33–37)* some of the disciples had been arguing on the road as to who was the greatest. Jesus challenged their preoccupation with ambition, because they were so far from understanding the true meaning of his Messiahship. This is why he used children to make an example of his followers in Capernaum. He challenged their ignorance and feelings of self-importance, saying:

'. . . If anyone wants to be first, he must be the very last, and the servant of all.' (Mark 9:35)

Status and rank may have been significant in Jewish thinking, but this was not what the Lord valued. What's more, Jesus used an infant not just to indicate that the disciples should serve 'lowly people' like children, but also that they should copy their example. This is brought out in Matthew's Gospel:

'And he said: "I tell you the truth, unless you change and become like little children, you will never enter the kingdom of heaven" . . .' *(Matthew 18:3)*

So why was Jesus indignant with his disciples in both chapters 9 and 10 of Mark's Gospel? Well, perhaps they just hadn't realised how much he cherished children. That's why he humbled his friends in front of the crowd. He was clearly reminding each one of them that they still hadn't got him all worked out! The fact that the disciples rebuked those who brought the children to Jesus suggests that they were not only protecting Jesus in his tiredness, but that other concerns were present. Could it be that they didn't think it was appropriate for those who were too young to understand his teaching to be making an acquaintance with him? Or, heaven forbid, could it be that the children concerned were the offspring of those who didn't follow Jesus? We don't know. All we read is that the Teacher made his point in word and deed: He *told* everyone present how significant children are to him: *'. . . the kingdom of God belongs to such as these.'* In other words, the kingdom belongs to those who will receive it as a free gift, like a child. It isn't about good works, or status, or keeping laws, but trustfulness and an open heart. Jesus then *demonstrated* how much he treasured this receptive quality, by sweeping the children into his arms and blessing them. The Lord placed a higher worth on innocence than a 'know it all' attitude. He honoured humility over pride, and trust over cynicism.

A Prayer

Bless me as I read, Lord,
that I may be open to your Spirit.
However important I may, or may not be;
whether I have kept your commands, or not;
no matter what ambition lies in my heart;
regardless of the quality of my service
or the depth of my learning –
speak to me through the honesty and purity of children.
Help me to listen and reflect.
Let my thoughts wander where they will,
but through my pondering
may the breath of your Spirit enable me to glimpse a vision of
    your kingdom.

Loving Saviour, may I know your arms embracing me Like A
   Child
and blessing me with the wisdom and warmth of your love.
Thank you, Lord. Amen.

Jesus said:
*'Ask and it will be given to you; seek and you will find; knock and
the door will be opened to you. For everyone who asks receives; he
who seeks finds; and to him who knocks, the door will be opened.
"Which of you, if his son asks for bread, will give him a stone? Or
if he asks for a fish, will give him a snake? If you, then, though
you are evil, know how to give good gifts to your children, how
much more will your Father in heaven give good gifts to those
who ask him!" ' (Matthew 7:7–11)*

AT HOME

'It is a wise father that knows his own child.'

William Shakespeare (1564–1616) –
The Merchant of Venice

1: 'Daddy, Where Are You?'

Jonathan (three years)

I was in the garden with Jonathan. As he'd put it: 'We're doing working.' I'd given him all the instructions; he was busy helping with a rake and enthusiastically getting the job done – well, almost! He was having a whale of a time – lost in a world of his own.

All was fine, until I bent down behind a bush to wrestle with a determined weed. It was then that Jonathan looked over his shoulder for reassurance and discovered Daddy was nowhere to be seen. Thinking he was alone and abandoned, he froze in panic. Tears trickled down his little face and he ran towards the house screaming, 'Daddy, where are you? Don't leave me out here!'

Of course, I still had my eye on him. I jumped up and ran towards him, sweeping him into my arms. 'It's all right,' I said, 'I'm here. Daddy wouldn't leave you alone.'

I learnt a lesson that day: There are times when I get so carried away with the busyness of life, that I lose sight of my Heavenly Father. I panic. I feel abandoned in the midst of life's circumstances: lost in a lonely world – needing reassurance. It's at times like these, when God seems to be hiding, that I must learn to cry out to him: *'My God, my God, why have you forsaken me?'* (Matthew 27:46b)

After all, that's what Jesus did – and, somehow, like him, I don't think I'll be disappointed in the end.

Bible Readings:

Jesus cries out to his Father	Matthew 27:45–54
The Great Commission	Matthew 28:16–20
Nothing can separate us	Romans 8:35–39

A Prayer

Faithful God,
when I feel abandoned and alone,
help me to cry out to you in all honesty.
Assure me of your loving presence,
and may your everlasting arms embrace and comfort me.
In Jesus' name, I pray. Amen.

2: 'It Wasn't Me!'

Hannah (six years) Jonathan (four years)

The back door opened and Hannah burst into the kitchen with tears running down her face. It was shortly afterwards that her brother defiantly made an entrance. In order to find out what happened, Mum tried in vain to listen to both of their indignant voices at the same time! Eventually, the noise level lowered and Jonathan summed up the situation whilst waving something in his hand: 'I didn't really hit Hannah with this big sharp stick!'

One of the things you don't have to teach children is to be naughty. It can be almost comical as you watch a young boy trying to get away with something, especially when he hasn't quite worked out how to deceive his parents effectively. It's when a little face has to avoid looking you in the eye that it becomes obvious that a cover up is being devised. On this occasion, Jonathan's defence was amusing, but transparently dishonest.

I learnt a lesson that day: Hiding the truth from others is something that everyone does at sometime or other. In fact, my deception as an adult can be quite effective. My experience of life has caused me to be more sophisticated and maybe even more successful in the way in which I hide truth from others. To be honest, it's a trick I can easily master. Yet, even if I develop the skill of pulling the wool over other people's eyes, I believe I can't fool God. He can see that proverbial *big sharp stick* that I'm hiding behind my back. So, the question is, can I comfortably look God in the eye, as it were? If not, I need to learn, like a child, to come and tell him all about it and receive his forgiveness.

Bible Readings:

A son deceives his father	Genesis 27:1–46
A warning for all	Acts 5:1–11
Practical advice for daily living	James 4:1–17

A Prayer

Merciful God,
I know that I often let you down through my dishonesty
and failure to own up to my wrongdoing.
I praise you for Jesus, who died that I might be forgiven.
Through him you offer me new life and a new beginning.
Help me to share the good news of your compassion with others
and may your Spirit raise up people of integrity,
who are not afraid to be truthful, fair and sincere in all they do.
May your kingdom come,
through Jesus Christ the Lord. Amen.

3: To the Rescue

Hannah (three years)

I was leading a Christian Basics class at home on a Sunday afternoon. Suddenly, Frances burst into the lounge and apologised for interrupting the group. She explained that our daughter had locked herself in the upstairs bathroom. Frances had tried talking her out, but Hannah couldn't work out how to open the door. The class found it very funny, until we realised that there wasn't an easy solution to the problem. In the end, I had to abandon the group and make my way upstairs, flanked by a couple of eager spectators (sorry – problem solvers!).

We decided that it was impossible to put a ladder up to the open window from outside because the patio roof was in the way. So, the only way to get Hannah out was to slide a short ladder out from the spare bedroom window, which was at a right angle to the toilet window. What followed had to be seen to be believed. I managed to bridge the gap between the two windowsills with the ladder and climbed out – still wearing my dog collar! I slowly made my way across, all the time reassuring Hannah and the members of the class who were all set to call an ambulance. Well, it wasn't an easy rescue, but in the end I managed to set my little girl free.

I learnt a lesson that day: Talking can often be limited in its effect. There are times when it takes a risky demonstration of love to drive the point home, or to solve a problem. Christians believe that God entered the world in human

24

form. In Jesus, he came to bridge the gap between himself and humanity: Jesus laid down his life to set people free from the captivity of selfishness and godlessness. The question is – are people happy to be rescued, like Hannah, and to welcome the arrival of a Saviour?

On that occasion, I was delighted to have accomplished my mission and those downstairs were thankful too. We all learnt an unexpected lesson through a real-life parable.

Bible Readings:

Jesus bridges the gap	Ephesians 2:11–18
True freedom	John 8:31–36
The Lord is our help and deliverer	Psalm 40

A Prayer

O God of deliverance,
I praise you that you loved the world so much,
that you sent your Son, Jesus.
He alone enables your children to be reconciled to you
and to one another.
May I know your freedom in my heart
and receive life eternal through Christ, my Saviour. Amen.

4: Nine Out of Ten Kids Prefer Not To!

Hannah (six years)

'Does cat food smell horrible to stop children eating it?' asked Hannah after she'd just given a spoonful of the smelly stuff to our cat for breakfast. I had to think twice before I gave the answer; it was quite an astute question for that time in the morning. It was later that same day that Hannah overheard some pretty graphic and awful news on the radio about a senseless killing in America. She'd started asking questions about that as well. I hadn't even realised she was listening at the time, let alone that she'd understood what was being said and was worrying about it.

I learnt a lesson that day: It might not be true for cat food, but we certainly take measures to stop children from consuming things that are not good for them: take child-locks and child-resistant bottle tops, for example. Yet, do I take as much care in protecting my children's eyes, ears and minds from disturbing images and news of wickedness in the world? Of course, I wouldn't want to wrap them up in cotton wool. They have to live in a real world and I should prepare them for it too. However, there are occasions when I think it's right to protect their innocence and shield them from that which could harm them.

Now, if that's true for children, then am I, as a child of God, protecting *myself* from unnecessary harmful influences? Do I set myself standards when I watch films, read books and listen to conversations? Wickedness in the world can be very subtle and doesn't come equipped with a horrible smell to make me realise what's bad for my spiritual appetite.

From my reading of the Bible *(Philippians 4:8)*, I believe I'm called to feast on whatever is true, whatever is noble, whatever is right, whatever is pure, whatever is lovely, whatever is admirable, and anything that's excellent or praiseworthy. If I do that, I'll develop a taste for what is wholesome and good for me. Something to think about when I next feed the cat!

Bible Readings:

Guard your hearts and minds	Philippians 4:4–9
Jesus prays for his disciples	John 17:6–19
Clean hands and a pure heart	Psalm 24:1–6

A Prayer

Good Lord,
help me to live in the real world, but as a faithful disciple.
Keep me safe, that I may not wander from your pathway,
and create in me a clean heart and an appetite for what is
      wholesome and pure.
Protect all who are vulnerable and innocent by the power of
      your Name,
that your peace, which transcends human understanding,
may be known in this world. Amen.

5: Comforter

Jonathan (five years)

I was delayed by the phone, which meant that I was very late for a meeting. 'Hurry up,' said Frances, 'It's nearly a quarter to eight!' I leapt into action, but just as I got to the top of the stairs, the zip on my briefcase broke and all my papers (I mean *all* my papers) fell out and floated down the stairs. I couldn't believe it. There must've been about 50 neatly ordered A4 sheets, ready for a presentation I was about to give. What's more, in haste, I hadn't numbered the pages – 'Lord give me patience, but give it to me now!' I wasn't in a good mood. There were sighs and tuts and expressions of despair. It was as I was pairing up the most crucial sheets, that I noticed Jonathan standing calmly by my side. His mouth was wide open at the sight and there was concern on his brow: 'Can I help you Dad?' he said, sensing the tension in the air. Frances proceeded to help me put things together and to bring order out of the chaos. Throughout this time, apart from making the helpful observation that, 'I ought to fix that zip,' Jonathan just sat down and watched with loving concern. In those moments his very presence was a calming influence. When all was done, he didn't say much, but he opened the front door for me and smiled.

I learnt a lesson that day: In the midst of the frantic rush, I believe God came alongside me in the form of a little boy and I felt the smile of his love. I'm reminded that the Holy Spirit of God is called the *Paraclete* (the Comforter). When life's out of control and a mess, when I forget God and struggle on my own, I believe his Spirit can gently give me the help I need – if only I wait on him. The trouble is, I'm often so blinkered that I don't recognise the presence of the Comforter beside me, one who's trying to tell me something and who can give me a new perspective on things.

So, I must watch out! It may be the Spirit of God will speak to me through someone today. What's more, if I'm filled with the Spirit, God can also speak to others through me – as I come alongside them in *their* need. A comforting thought and calmly written – thanks to Jonathan!

Bible Readings:

Jesus calms the storm	Mark 4:35–41
Jesus promises the Holy Spirit	John 14:15–27
Waiting for the Father's gift	Acts 1:1–8

A Prayer

Forgive me, Lord,
for those times when I lose my cool;
when I mess up, because I let the busyness of life take control.
I thank you,
that you come alongside me by your Spirit.
Help me to recognise the smile of your love in others
and, for the sake of your kingdom,
use even me to bring comfort and help to others. Amen.

6: Honest to God

Jonathan (five years)

'What kids need today is plenty of LSD.' What? I couldn't believe what I was reading until I finished the sentence: 'LSD . . . Love, Security and Discipline.' These qualities won't give children a *high* all the time, but I'm sure they'll lead to a more lasting happiness.

It reminds me of the occasion when Jonathan had been misbehaving and was consequently sent to his room. After the time came for him to be allowed downstairs again, he descended with heavy feet and a really stern look on his little face. Staring straight at me, he said, 'I'm really cross with you Dad, but I still love you!' His words took me by surprise. I didn't expect him to tell me he loved me at that precise moment! What's more, he'd pinched *my* line!

I learnt a lesson that day: As I thought about Jonathan's words, 'I'm really cross with you, but I still love you!', I can imagine my Heavenly Father saying the same thing to me at times. So often I must hurt and even anger him with my disobedience and selfishness. Yet, he never stops loving his children perfectly; he just longs for us all to take responsibility for our lives and to acknowledge our shortcomings. In other words, he wants me to be prepared to make changes in my life with his help and to receive the forgiveness that Jesus has made possible.

It took a five-year-old to help me realise that God's ways can often be difficult to understand. His discipline can be hard to accept and sometimes he really does move in a mysterious way. If I'm honest, there are times I find myself saying to God, 'I'm really cross with you, Lord!' Yet, just as Jonathan won't always understand why his Dad behaves as he does, it's natural for a child of God to be bemused and angry with *him* too. Nevertheless, I believe he still loves me, even though I get cross with him at times. So, in the midst of all my confusion, perhaps I should take a leaf out of Jonathan's book and still love my Heavenly Father and be honest with him. I guess: 'Love is . . . a two way thing!'

Bible Readings:

Slow to anger, abounding in love	Psalm 86
Do you love me?	John 21:15–19
Forgive as the Lord forgave you	Colossians 3:12–17

A Prayer

God of mystery,
there is so much I don't understand.
Help me to trust in your constant and perfect love.
I'm sorry for those times when I get angry with you.
I really do love you!
Forgive and be patient with me.
Assure me of your love for me and all humanity,
through your Son and my Lord, Jesus Christ. Amen.

7: 'Oh Yes He Is!'

Hannah (four years)

It was my rest day and I was in the Manse garden (affectionately called 'The Conservation Area'). Now, I'm not particularly good at gardening, but it's quite therapeutic to get outside and to hack away at a few weeds – there are usually plenty to choose from!

I'd just got into a rhythm when someone called at the door. In the distance I could see a bright yellow anorak through the frosted glass. I knew exactly who it was; let's call him 'Micky': a young lad who'd become rather dependent on me as his minister. He was forever on the doorstep asking for help concerning *something and nothing*. Fortunately for me, Frances responded to the sound of the bell, but was a little disheartened as Micky asked yet again, 'Is the minister in?' Hesitantly, she asked if it was urgent. As always, it was. Frances decided to protect my space saying, 'I'm sorry, could you call tomorrow? Tony's not in the house at the moment.' I breathed a sigh of relief in the garden, impressed by Frances' quick thinking. Then, all of a sudden, I heard young Hannah shouting, 'Oh yes he is! Dad's here in the garden, Mummy – I'll get him!' Don't you just love children sometimes!

I learnt a lesson that day: People need time for themselves. Of course it's right that I should make time for rest and leisure. After all, even Jesus took time out from his ministry to be away from the crowds *and* he had the whole world to save. Yet, I can't help but feel that God sometimes uses those unwelcome interruptions to a comfortable routine for his purposes. Those words of Jesus are so challenging: '. . . whatever you did not do for one of the least of these, you did not do for me.' (Matthew 25:45) We might not know who it is that's knocking at the door, but you can be sure there's someone who does!

Bible Readings:

Love one another	1 John 3:11–24
Sheep and goats	Matthew 25:31–46
The Judge stands at the door	James 5:7–12

A Prayer

Forgive me, Lord,
for when you knocked on my door today, I didn't know it was
*   you.*
Help me not to be resentful,
but to give myself in love as you have commanded.
When my comfortable routine is interrupted,
may I discern the whisper of your Spirit
and find your will for my life in work, devotion and even in
*   leisure.*
When I am tired and need space,
guide me to the place of refreshment and renewal
that you have prepared for me and those that I love dearly.
Thank you, Lord. Amen.

Speak to us of Children

And a woman who held a babe against her bosom said,
Speak to us of children.
And he said:
Your children are not your children.
They are the sons and daughters of Life's longing for itself.
They come through you but not from you,
And though they are with you yet they belong not to you.

You may give them your love but not your thoughts,
For they have their own thoughts.
You may house their bodies but not their souls,
For their souls dwell in the house of tomorrow,
which you cannot visit, not even in your dreams.
You may strive to be like them, but seek not to make them like you.
For life goes not backward nor tarries with yesterday.
You are the bows from which your children as living arrows are sent forth.
The Archer sees the mark upon the path of the infinite,
And He bends you with His might that His arrows may go swift and far.
Let your bending in the Archer's hand be for gladness;
For even as He loves the arrow that flies, so He loves also the bow that is
*   stable.*

From 'The Prophet' by Kahlil Gibran (1883–1931)

AT SCHOOL

'When I was a boy of fourteen my father was so ignorant I could hardly stand to have him around. But when I got to be twenty-one, I was astonished at how much he had learned in seven years.'

Mark Twain (1835–1910)

8: Straight to the Top!

Hannah (five years)

Some time ago, in the midst of dashing to get ready for infant school, Hannah asked me a serious question: 'You're a minister Daddy. Why haven't you taken our school assembly before?' It was a bad moment to ask. Impatiently and without thinking, I said that I didn't know why and she should ask her teachers – not me! I then pleaded with her to put her coat on and get moving. Eventually, she raced off with Mum.

Later that day, Hannah went striding up to her Headmistress (or her 'head mischief' as she sometimes called her!). Fearlessly, and probably with hands on hips, she said, 'Why haven't you asked my Daddy to take assembly with his puppet, because we haven't had him before?' Well, in the afternoon, the 'head mischief', sorry, 'mistress', rang me apologetically, explaining that Hannah had reprimanded her. She then enthusiastically booked me for Harvest. We had a giggle and I accepted her warm invitation. A little girl's impulsive action achieved a great deal and I was very proud of her.

I learnt a lesson that day: At times, I can be very slow to take action – even when I feel passionately about something. Often, I lack courage, or the motivation to go straight to the top and say what I think as a Christian. Yet, there are so many important issues that need to be addressed. Perhaps I ought to be more of a *mischief*-maker, for the sake of the kingdom of God – after all, wasn't Jesus?

36

Bible Readings:

A servant girl's boldness	2 Kings 5:1–14
The faith of the Centurion	Luke 7:1–10
Jesus makes his views known	Mark 11:15–18

A Prayer

Living God,
may I never be complacent.
Grant me the strength to stand up for what I believe in,
wisdom to know what to say and do,
and courage to face the consequences.
May I follow Jesus' example,
for the sake of your kingdom. Amen.

9: 'What's Early?'

Infant school playground

A young mum arrived outside the school and breathlessly chatted with my wife, Frances. She was admitting that it was a struggle to get her four-year-old daughter to nursery on time. She was despairing of the fact that she had a young baby who always seemed to need a feed, or a nappy change, just at the wrong moment! Of course, there were all the other things that had to be done too. She went on to say that there was one occasion when they actually got to nursery school in good time! On arriving, with relief she had said, 'Oh, we're really early!' Without hesitation her daughter replied, 'What's *'early'*, Mummy?'

I expect the little girl wouldn't have had to ask what the word *'late'* meant. Her mum admitted she was always saying: 'Come on, we really must get going!'

I learnt a lesson that day: If I'm not careful, I can spend my life dashing here and there and everywhere. My daily routine can become set against the clock with little room to breathe or enjoy the precious moments God has given me. Rather, I allow myself to be put under tremendous pressure.

It's true that family life will always make demands upon people. There are also countless other things that will complicate life. It's easy to become taken over by events and distractions.

Frances and I lose count of the number of times we say *'We're late'* to our children. I wonder what God thinks about our crazy lifestyles? One day will he point out to us that we missed so much because we were always too busy, too late, or too distracted? Perhaps I need to try and take greater control over my life. If not, will I find that I'm *too* late, because I'd never learnt to be in good time for Jesus – the greatest teacher of all?

Bible Readings:

Use of time	Luke 10:38–42
Making time	Mark 1:29–39
Be still	Psalm 46

A Prayer

Ever patient God,
what must you think of my lifestyle?
So often I am worried and upset over many things,
my life is set against the clock
and there are never enough hours in the day.
Help me to be still and know that you are God,
to take control of my life and seek what you would have me do,
in the name of Jesus Christ, my teacher. Amen.

10: 'When I Grow Up . . .'

Hannah (seven years) Jonathan (five years)

My children were just at that age where their dad was looked up to and bragged about in the infant school playground: 'My daddy's church is the biggest in the whole world!' Well, it certainly made me feel good, even if it wasn't true. On another occasion, Hannah asked her mum, 'Does Daddy know Tony Blair?' She thought I knew everybody. Jonathan even thought that he would be called Tony when he became a dad! 'And, when I grow up,' he said, 'I'm going to be a *sitting down minister!*' – referring to the fact that he wanted to be a preacher like me, but didn't fancy standing for the whole service!

Another lovely story is when Jonathan said to a friend, 'What's your daddy? Is he a minister, or a fireman, or what?' Then came the reply with a shrug, 'No, he's just a man!'

I learnt a lesson that day: There are a few years in a child's life when parents, or carers, may be seen as 'the best in the world' and they can do no wrong in their eyes. All this is good for the ego, but soon children reach the age of enlightenment and their parents miraculously transform into nothing but an embarrassment. Well, I suppose it's important that my offspring realise that I'm 'just a man' and not perfect: hopefully a loveable, caring father, but someone who, *like a child*, needs a role model too.

So, who might that be? Well, as I grow in faith, I simply want to become more like Jesus. He's someone who's really worth looking up to. I believe he wasn't 'just a man' like me. He *was*, and *is*, God's Son – sent from my Heavenly Father. Yet, in him I find a perfect example of humanity – one who really is 'the best in the world' – and beyond it too!

Bible Readings:

Fix your thoughts on Jesus	Hebrews 3:1–6
Jesus calls the first disciples	Matthew 4:18–22
Aim for perfection	2 Corinthians 13:5–14

A Prayer

Father God,
I would like to be as good as other people may think I am.
Yet, I ask you to ensure that I fulfil your expectations for my
    life, not theirs.
May I fix my eyes and thoughts upon Jesus, your Son,
who alone is perfect and worthy of the greatest honour.
As I seek to follow him,
help me by your Spirit to be the best that I can be,
for the sake of your kingdom and those who look up to me.
    Amen.

11: The Show Must Go On!

Hannah (seven years)

Hannah was dancing in her school concert. It was a performance to mark her move from the infants' into the juniors'. All the parents had gathered obediently in the school hall, trying not to look daft perched on tiny little chairs. They were nervously clutching their cameras and there was a tremendous atmosphere as everyone anticipated the arrival of the children. When they eventually emerged, they looked so innocent in their cute costumes, bearing smiles that revealed missing teeth. The children had been practising hard, learning their lines and, of course, the stage directions too!

The end result was an angelic treat, bringing a tear and smile to us all. Yet, there was one particular aspect that fascinated me. After the preparation, all the anticipation, and despite the vast gathering of parents, some children still managed to switch into a world of their own: captivated by the fly at the window, the irresistible thumb to suck, or the antics of a toddler in the audience. They easily became distracted in mid-sentence, or even in mid-song. It was so funny to watch.

In contrast, there were others who kept on going, come what may. One boy even managed to carry on singing when the pocket watch he was spinning flew off its chain! Little Ian knew what he had to do, and nothing was going to stop him.

I learnt a lesson that day: At times I lose *my* concentration too. I can so easily become distracted from the part

God has called me to play as a Christian in the world. Temptations cause me to switch my focus, when all the time there are people watching to see if I'm serious about my faith. Whilst I know I don't have to live up to their expectations, I do need to remember the God in the gallery who *does* matter! Little Ian taught me that the 'show must go on!', for I've been chosen to play the part that God the great Producer and Director has given me.

Bible Readings:

Standing firm against temptation   1 Corinthians 10:12–13
A call to persevere   Hebrews 10:19–25
Stephen keeps his focus to the end Acts 6:8–7:60

A Prayer

God, the great Producer and Director,
help me to keep my focus on Jesus,
who was the broadcaster of your word
and also the message.
May I resist the temptation
to become distracted in the performance of my duties.
Rather, let me play my part
in the power of your Spirit of creativity. Amen.

12: God's Gang

Hannah (seven years)

In the school playground, there always seems to be a new craze of one sort or another. Yet, the good old *Yoyo* lives up to its name and keeps making a comeback. When Hannah was seven, nearly everyone seemed to have one. Children were busy in their gangs, practising their skills and performing tricks – like 'walking the dog' and 'round the world'. I soon became an expert in the jargon. For me, it became quite a change from feeding or exercising *Tamagotchis* while my children were at school.

Yet, there seemed to be a problem even with the harmless Yoyo. Those who didn't possess one were really left out. What's more, there was the pressure to have a bigger, brighter and faster one than anyone else. On one occasion, Hannah returned from school really upset. Sadly, her friends wouldn't play with her because she didn't have one of her own. As they weren't too expensive, Mum scoured the town and eventually found a shop that still had Yoyos in stock. Hannah was happy again. She enthusiastically took her posh *ProYo* to school, with strict instructions not to ignore, or tease, those who weren't so fortunate: 'Remember how you felt, Hannah!'

I learnt a lesson that day: As an adult, I can be so busy trying to keep up with the latest fads and fashions, and so dependent on material security, that it can make me self-centred. I can find I'm failing to love and care for those who are less fortunate than myself. Like a child, I must learn to love people for who they are, rather than for what they have, whom they know, or even how they look. I'm challenged by the fact that one day I'll be held to account for what I do with all that I possess, and the way I treat people. So, whilst I thank God that his love doesn't depend on how many Yoyos I've got, or how impressive or skilful I am, I do need to remember that it's not always easy being in God's Gang!

Bible Readings:

God doesn't judge by appearances	Galatians 2:6–10
Do not show favouritism	James 2:1–13
God calls lowly Gideon	Judges 6:1–24

A Prayer

Merciful God,
your love is eternally deep and never shallow.
Your knowledge of me is perfect
and you never judge people superficially.
I thank you that you are interested in my heart and who I am,
and not about my status or possessions.
Help me to reflect your generous nature
and not to show favouritism.
May I act justly, love mercy and walk humbly in faith,
and so be recognised and known as a loyal member of your
   Gang. Amen.

13: 'I'm Special!'

Jonathan (five years)

Jonathan was walking home from infant school and chatting ten to the dozen with his friend Matthew. They were discussing their forthcoming Harvest festival, excited because their parents had been invited to attend. 'I'm going to be a reader,' said Jonathan proudly. 'Are you?' replied Matthew, and instantly he responded with, 'That's good, I'm going to be a clapper!' Then, off they went on their way, skipping happily down the road together.

I learnt a lesson that day: Two small boys had accepted each other's roles and, what's more, were genuinely pleased for each other. We all have something to offer, whether it be a natural gift, the ability to be part of a team, or simply a quality in our character. Jonathan's Harvest wouldn't work if there were just readers at the front. There were other essential parts to be played for the act of worship to be complete. In the Bible, St Paul says a Christian community will only function properly if every member knows that they've a special job to do, and appreciates that everyone is important.

It reminds me of the story of three siblings who were asked if they were helpful to their mum and dad at home. The eldest one said, 'I do the washing up.' The second child added, 'I dry the dishes.' Then the youngest one said, 'And I pick up all the broken ones!' An important job too!

So, whenever I'm feeling inadequate or worthless; when I'm tempted to believe I've nothing to offer, I need to remember that God needs me to bring a harmony to the world. For without you and me, his great symphony of life would be unfinished.

Bible Readings:

A special job for a young man	Jeremiah 1:4–10
A most reluctant leader	Exodus 4:8–17
Many parts, but one body	1 Corinthians 12:7–31

A Prayer

Forgive me, Lord, when I think that I'm a nobody;
when I'm tempted to believe that I'm useless
and no good to anyone.
Help me to remember that I am special to you – unique!
You didn't intend there to be another me,
for another me is not necessary.
May I be true to myself
and play the part you have created for me.
By your Spirit, release my gifts,
and assure me of your love and purpose for my life. Amen.

14: A Comic Relief

Hannah (seven years)

Hannah went to school dressed in red from head to toe. She was also wearing a tartan cap with artificial blonde plaits coming from underneath it. This wasn't the introduction of a new uniform, but Hannah's effort to enter into the spirit of Red Nose Day. All the children and staff had been given permission to dress up for the occasion. Later that day, Hannah was sitting in class when a teacher came into the room and asked her to come and see the Headteacher. Now, my daughter obviously had a guilty conscience because, when telling the story, she said that her immediate thought was, 'I hope I haven't been naughty, like bullying, or something like that!' Once outside the class, she was joined by some other pupils and the Headteacher. There was some *comical relief* when they realised they'd only been summoned because they had the best costumes in the school. Hannah's worry turned to joy and delight. There was much excitement as those gathered were told that their photo was going to be taken and would appear in the local paper.

I learnt a lesson that day: I was impressed by Hannah's enthusiasm to raise money for those in need and also her understanding of what Red Nose Day was aiming to achieve. It made me think about my own response to the poor and needy in the world: am I really a 'cheerful giver?' I felt deeply challenged. One day, at the end of my earthly life, I believe I'll meet the greatest Teacher of all face to face. When that time comes, would I justifiably have a guilty conscience? Or would my Lord praise me for my sacrificial giving? I'm glad that he is just and forgiving. Nevertheless, I still have a responsibility to the people of Africa and the poorer nations of the planet.

Could it be that Jesus is seeing *red* at the injustices of the world, but smiles when children and adults show a little compassion and support worthy causes like Red Nose Day?

Bible Readings:

A salutary tale for the rich	Luke 16:19–31
The believers help those in need	Acts 4:32–37
Give generously to the poor	Deuteronomy 15:1–11

A Prayer

Jehovah Jireh – my provider!
You have given me so much,
especially through my Lord and Saviour, Jesus.
With open hands and a thankful heart,
may I give to those in need –
cheerfully, generously and unconditionally!
Soften my hardened heart with your grace and compassion,
for the sake of your kingdom's justice. Amen.

Children Learn What They Observe

A child who lives with criticism,
learns to condemn.
A child who lives with hostility,
learns to fight.
A child who lives with ridicule,
learns to be shy.
A child who lives with shame,
learns to feel guilty.
A child who lives with tolerance,
learns to be patient.
A child who lives with encouragement,
learns confidence.
A child who lives with praise,
learns to appreciate.
A child who lives with fairness,
learns justice.
A child who lives with security,
learns to have faith.
A child who lives with approval,
learns to like himself or herself.
A child who lives with acceptance and friendship,
learns to find love in the world.

Anonymous

AT CHURCH OR PRAYER

'Was Jesus called Master because he wasn't married?'

Hannah Miles (six years)

15: 'Speak Clearly, Please!'

Carolyn (seven years) – friend of Hannah and Jonathan

Someone once said, 'An unusual child is one who asks parents questions they *can* answer.' Life is never dull when young children enter the age of asking 'Why?' all the time. Like the little girl, Carolyn, who after a church service asked me, 'Why is God called Peter?' I wasn't quite sure where to start. Before I had time to say anything, she went on to say, 'I know God's first name is Peter, because that's what you call him!' I was puzzled, until Carolyn carefully explained that at the end of every Holy Communion service I say, 'Thanks *Peter* God!' Well, an easy mistake to make.

Rather like the child who thought God's name was 'Harold', because he'd heard Christians praying, 'Our Father, *Harold* be thy name . . . '

Moreover, what about the children who've spent time in church looking for the *'Prairie Tortoise'* – only to find that the minister actually said, '. . . and now, the prayer he taught us!'

I learnt a lesson that day: We may laugh, but Carolyn made me realise I need to speak clearly about my Christian faith: in a language people can understand! Otherwise, what I say could be meaningless.

It's helpful when children ask what 'Amen' means, for example. When they do, they probably speak for many adults who haven't a clue either. I've come to realise that it's not very clever to use Christian jargon without explanation, or to communicate faith in a sloppy way. Perhaps I ought to pay attention to the words of the Master Communicator – Jesus! He chose his words so very carefully. He was relevant and spoke clearly and simply too. For that: 'Thanks be to God!'

Bible Readings:

Paul's instructions   Colossians 4:2–6
Clearly written commands   Deuteronomy 27:1–8
                                   Any of Jesus' parables

A Prayer

Creator God,
thank you for the gift of humour,
for the ability to communicate
and for all that helps me learn and understand.
As I read the Bible,
equip me to speak clearly and simply about my faith,
for the sake of those who don't know my Lord and Saviour.
  Amen.

16: Daddy

Jonathan (one year)

The church was packed full and I was conducting a service of Holy Communion. I'd dusted down my best clerical garb and really looked the part. There was a hush of expectation in the air as I removed the white cloth covering the bread and wine. Then, with great joy and faith, I exclaimed, 'Lift up your hearts!' Well, before the congregation could respond with, 'We lift them to the Lord!' a one-year-old baby cried out *'Daddy!'*

I'm glad it was *my* son, and I couldn't help wearing a broad smile. The congregation laughed spontaneously and my wife, who was holding him, went bright red. Jonathan had just been brought into the church from the crèche. He'd seen his daddy and simply wanted to call out to me – just as he'd do when I'm at home in jeans and a sweatshirt. It made no difference that I was dressed in a black cassock and leading a dignified service in front of 200 people.

I learnt a lesson that day: Jesus came to show people that the Almighty Creator can also be known as a loving Heavenly Father. He taught his disciples to pray to God as *'Abba'*, which means, *'Daddy'*. Of course, it's important that I never lose sight of the awesome majesty and holiness of God. He is worthy of all my worship, honour and respect. Yet, in a mysterious way, Jesus taught me that it's possible to have an intimate relationship with my Father: one closer than that between a good human parent and child.

In Psalm 8:2 the Psalmist praises God: *'From the lips of*

children and infants you have ordained praise . . .' I hope, out of well-meaning piety, I never insist that children should be *seen* but not *heard* in church. The truth is, they have too much to teach me about God my Father!

Bible Readings:

How should we pray?	Matthew 6:5–13
God's love for Israel	Hosea 11:1–11
Spirit of sonship	Romans 8:15–17

A Prayer

Abba Father,
you are a powerful Creator
and yet you love and care for me.
You know me better than I know myself,
but still you have time for me.
May I have time for children
And, in humility, learn from them.
I put my trust in you,
through Jesus Christ, my Lord. Amen.

17: How Sweet the Name

Hannah (six years) Jonathan (four years)

It was reported in the *Church Times* that, after visiting a church in Melton Mowbray, a child wrote in her school essay, 'The difference between the Church of England and the Methodist Church is that the Methodist Church has double glazing.' Oh that things were that simple!

Young children say what they see. Hannah and Jonathan used to describe their church as *'Daddy's church'* – not too surprising as I'm the minister. In the same vein they identified the other churches in the area: the *'Kath Lick church'* was labelled the *'party church'*: not because it was charismatic, but rather they'd been to lots of parties in the church hall there. The Parish church became *'Father Christmas' church'*: logical as Santa visited their Christmas Fayre. Moreover, on one occasion, they were looking forward to going to the *'Firework church'* because they were on their way to a fabulous display there for bonfire night.

I learnt a lesson that day: As we watched fireworks and reflected on Hannah and Jonathan's list of *'Churches Together – according to the Miles'*, I realised that it's crucial that Christians recognise that people often have an image of the Church that's inaccurate, or sadly lacking. It's not always the fault of the Christian community, but sometimes it is. How would I describe many of the churches I know? What adjectives would a child use? It's worth a thought.

The Church should be seen as a community of love. Jesus pointed out that his disciples would be known by their love for one another. *(John 13:35)* If there were more love, perhaps in essence there would be little difference between churches. I want my children to learn that it's not *'Daddy's church'*, but it belongs to Jesus – the King of love!

Bible Readings:

Building together	Romans 15:1–7
Jesus' prayer for us	John 17:20–26
A new commandment	John 13:31–38

A Prayer

Prince of Peace,
you prayed that those who believe in you should be one,
just as you are one with the Father;
yet, so often Christians let you down through unnecessary
    divisions.
I'm sure people of faith will always express themselves
    differently,
for you have made us rich in our diversity.
But bear with us Lord, despite our failings,
and lead us to a spirit of true unity.
May we build each other up through our fellowship in your
    Name,
and encourage one another as we share in your mission to the
    world. Amen.

18: Sorry Seems to be the Hardest Word

Hannah (seven years)

On the way home from Girls' Brigade, Frances asked our daughter what she'd been doing. Hannah replied, 'We were asked to write down a 'sorry' prayer to God in one sentence.' Intrigued, Mum said, 'Oh yes, and how did you get on?' 'Okay, except I wrote eight sentences!' Mother and daughter looked at each other and giggled. (They remembered an argument the night before, when Hannah had been duly reprimanded for her behaviour.) 'Oh, that would make a good *'Like A Child'* thought,' said Hannah. (If I'm not careful she'll be writing my scripts for me!)

I learnt a lesson that day: As Hannah shared her eight 'sorry' sentences she began to list them. For example:

1. Sorry for being cross with Mum . . .
3. Sorry for hitting my brother . . .
6. Sorry for saying: 'Go away' to my friend . . .

But, it was number seven that struck me: Sorry, God, for breaking your heart!

It was straight to the point and it made *me* think. How do *I* break God's heart? I may be conscious of his love and forgiveness, but do I honestly acknowledge my failings? Do I recognise the pain I must cause him?

Sir Elton John sings a song entitled, 'Sorry seems to be the hardest word' – it's probably true! It's difficult to swallow pride in humility before God, and other people. It can also be hard for parents to admit they're sometimes wrong to their children. So, back to Hannah's eight sentences: Frances explained that if we're sorry for our wrongdoing then, thanks to Jesus, God will forgive us. It's like rubbing out all the writing on the page and starting again. I'm proud of Hannah's honesty. The question is: How many sentences do *I* really need to write down today?

Bible Readings:

King David seeks forgiveness	Psalm 51
Confession and repentance	Matthew 3:1–12
From darkness to light	1 John 1:5–2:14

A Prayer

Gracious God,
it's comforting to know
that some of the great characters in the Bible made their
  mistakes too –
even King David and Peter the Rock.
I thank you that you love me despite my faults
and see the potential that is in me.
I humbly bring myself before you
with sorrow for my shortcomings and selfishness;
seeking forgiveness for my wrongdoing:
Create in me a clean heart, O God.
Renew a right spirit within me,
that I may walk in the light with my Lord and Saviour Jesus,
for his sake. Amen.

19: Shine, Jesus, Shine!

Hannah (seven years)

On Sundays, my children used to attend a swimming club. In fact, it coincided with our evening church service. One day, Frances was bringing the children home after a good swim. As they were coming towards the church, they looked to see if Daddy was in the pulpit and counted how many people were in the congregation. The front of our church is all glass, so everyone on the High Street can see what's going on inside. From across the road, Hannah peered in and then looked up above the church and said to her mum, 'We've only got half a cross!' She was quite right. Normally the cross on top of the spire shines brightly – cleverly illuminated using fibre optics. The trouble was, one of the bulbs had obviously blown.

I learnt a lesson that day: Hannah's observation reminded me of the words of Jesus to his followers: *'You are the light of the world. A city on a hill cannot be hidden. Neither do people light a lamp and put it under a bowl. Instead they put it on its stand, and it gives light to everyone in the house. In the same way, let your light shine before men, that they may see your good deeds and praise your Father in heaven.' (Matthew 5:14–16)* It made me think: when people look at me, do they see Jesus shining through? Are they struck by the love of the Lord in my life – his compassion, concern and holiness? In other words, does the light that shines from me show the *full* cross of Jesus, or only half of it?

My worship is important, but it isn't the whole picture.

The challenge is to put my faith into practice outside the church – that means making sacrifices. Through the prophet Isaiah, God said, '. . . *if you spend yourselves on behalf of the hungry and satisfy the needs of the oppressed, then your light will rise in the darkness, and your night will become like the noonday.' (Isaiah 58:10)* Hannah will be pleased that the cross above the church is now shining brightly again with the help of a new bulb. May the love of Jesus shine out of me with the help of the Holy Spirit!

Bible Readings:

Salt and light	Matthew 5:13–16
The right kind of fasting	Isaiah 58:6–12
Put on the armour of light	Romans 13:8–14

A Prayer

Light of the World,
I know that your love is the answer.
Help me to put aside the deeds of darkness
and to put on the armour of light.
As I love my neighbour as myself,
may your light be seen shining from me.
Jesus, you died that my life may be totally transformed.
I pray that, as I take up my cross in obedience,
I may know your help,
so that the fullness of your glory may radiate brightly,
for the sake of your kingdom. Amen.

20: Father's Eyes

Hannah (six years) Jonathan (four years)

I was chatting with someone after a church service. They remarked that my children must've got their big brown eyes from their mother. Well, I'm not disputing that, except that *other* people have attributed their good-looking eyes to their 'good-looking' father. Oh well, worth a try! The fact is, brown-eyed Mum *and* Dad have *both* got something to do with it. I expect most people can pinpoint distinctive characteristics, or mannerisms, that have been inherited from their parents.

I learnt a lesson that day: I asked myself the question: Have I got my Heavenly Father's eyes? I was reminded of the Christian singer, Amy Grant, and one of the gospel songs she recorded: *Father's Eyes* – taken from the album of the same name. The song is about a woman who wants to bear the characteristics of her creator, so that people say of her, 'Aren't you like your Heavenly Father!'

I wonder, who do people see in me? If it's not apparent that I'm a child of God, perhaps I should spend more time with him. For when I spend quality time in prayer, Bible study, and in fellowship with other believers, then the more I'll act like his Son, Jesus, and bear his likeness.

I'm really proud of the fact that my children look like their mum and dad – even though they may not thank us in years to come! Yet, one thing's for sure, true sons and daughters of God will never be disappointed by *his* beauty.

Bible Readings:

Being transformed into his likeness	2 Corinthians 3:7–18
The image of the invisible God	Colossians 1:9–20
Moses and the Glory of the Lord	Exodus 33:12–23
The radiant face of Moses	Exodus 34:29–35

A Prayer

Loving Father,
it's a wonderful thing to know I am your precious child.
As I look to you in my devotions,
help me to understand my heritage
and to bear your holy characteristics.
As people look into my eyes,
may they see your love and compassion,
that in some way I may reflect your image.
By your Grace,
transform me into the likeness of Jesus
with an ever-increasing glory. Amen.

21: No Need to Shout

Joshua (four years) – Hannah and Jonathan's cousin

It was early in the evening and my brother was settling his four-year-old son Joshua down for the night. As usual, Steve suggested that they say prayers together. On this occasion however, Josh made it clear that he didn't want to say his prayers. He was tired after a long day and he wasn't really in the right frame of mind. Reassuringly, Steve then explained that prayers didn't have to be said only at bedtime, because you can talk to Jesus whenever you are able: 'He's always listening.' Then Josh, with the wisdom of a child replied, 'Yes, and Jesus *never* says pardon!' What a lovely thought and quite correct, Josh!

I learnt a lesson that day: How often have I said my prayers and wondered if God is really listening? Sometimes, because of my circumstances, I've honestly felt that the Lord must be hard of hearing. However, deep down, I believe that prayers said in Jesus' name are always heard. God is attentive and never too busy. In fact, he knows me better than I know myself. That doesn't mean that my prayers are always answered exactly as I'd expect. I've learnt to trust that my Heavenly Father hears and answers all prayers according to his perfect will – not as I ask in my ignorance, nor as I deserve in my sinfulness, but as he knows and loves me. So, it doesn't matter when I pray, or where, or even how I'm feeling. He simply wants me to speak to him honestly and bring my praises and requests to him.

So, Josh is right, I don't have to shout, for Jesus never *says*: 'Pardon?' The only *pardon* on his lips is the kind he grants when I'm truly sorry and confess failures in love and prayer.

Bible Readings:

The prayer of faith	James 5:13–20
If my people pray	2 Chronicles 7:11–22
Nehemiah – a man of prayer	Nehemiah 1:1–2:5

A Prayer

Lord God,
I thank you that you are only a prayer away
and that you know what is on my heart even before I ask, or
*   think.*
Grant me an assurance that your ear is attentive to hear my
*   prayers day and night*
and that your eyes are open to see my situation.
Help me to seek your face and to turn towards you.
In doing so, may I know your love and forgiveness in my own
*   experience*
and discover that the prayer of the righteous is powerful and
*   effective,*
through Jesus Christ my Lord. Amen.

The Ministry of Children

Lord, your word has been presented to us by our children.
It has come to us through their words, their expressive gestures
and their manner of interpreting the gospel and the facts of life.
Little children are often considered
as beings that must only receive
and submit themselves to the power of big grown-ups.
People think they can give something
only on the sentimental level.
Instead, in bearing witness to life,
in the deeds, the expressions
and the drive towards high ideals of children and teenagers
we have to discover human values
indispensable for the path of history.
Moreover, the Christian community must discover here the
authentic proclamation of your word;
it must accept this human dialogue
which involves faith and life and calls for clear cut choices.
From now on we will try to consider children
as people capable of giving a notable contribution to society
and we want to give them room
in the community and in the neighbourhood.
This engagement is called for
because of important social reasons and,
for us, it also is evangelically inspired.
In fact, Jesus, thought very highly of children.
He considered them an essential component
of that world of the 'least' and 'the little ones'
upon which society, history and the Kingdom of God rest.
He made himself little
and fully subjected himself to poverty and partook in the
destiny of the masses at the bottom of society.

From the Isolotto Community, Latin America,
written with the help of children.
Found in *Now* magazine.
© Trustees for Methodist Church Purposes
Used with kind permission.

AT LARGE

'A mother walked into her son's bedroom and found the little boy tying a bandage round his finger. "My poor boy!" she exclaimed. "What have you done to your finger?" "I hit it with a hammer, Mummy." "But I didn't hear you crying, darling." "No – I thought you were out!"'

(Anonymous)

22: On Your Bike!

Hannah (six years)

I can vividly remember the day I learnt to ride a bike without stabilisers – I hasten to add that it was a long time ago! It was a major achievement and was the beginning of an adventure and a new found freedom. I recall when Hannah was about to take a step of faith and discard *her* stabilisers. She'd been down to just one extra wheel for a while, which had been fairly successful as long as she leant to the left and not to the right! Yet, Hannah would never really learn to ride until the remaining stabiliser was removed.

One day, Frances and I explained that learning to balance on a bike is rather like a baby learning to walk and take those first important steps. It will mean that you fall down a few times, but if you're determined to get up and try again, then you'll gradually gain confidence and skill.

I learnt a lesson that day: I remembered how, in the Bible, Peter tried to walk on the water. He was fine whilst he was looking ahead towards Jesus, but once he noticed the strong wind, he became afraid and started to sink down in the sea. In the same way, Hannah had to look ahead of herself when riding and not look behind her. It was so very tempting to look back when she passed something that had caught her eye, or made her nervous. Time and time again, I had to repeat, 'Look forwards and watch where you are going!'

I think there's a lesson here for me in my Christian faith.

I need to fix my eyes on Jesus so that I won't be swayed by all the distractions that inevitably surround me in my life. If I lose concentration and trust, I'm in danger of taking a fall. Although we can learn from our tumbles, the writer of the New Testament letter to the Hebrews wrote: *'Let us fix our eyes on Jesus, the author and perfecter of our faith . . .' (Hebrews 12:2).* It's Jesus who should be the focus for all Christians – certainly the stabilising factor I need in *my* life!

Bible Readings:

Jesus walks on the water	Matthew 14:22–33
Focused discipleship	Hebrews 12:1–13
Fix your gaze before you	Proverbs 4:20–27

A Prayer

Lord Jesus,
I know my walk with you is wobbly!
Forgive me for becoming so easily distracted
and for having such little faith.
Thank you for tending my wounds when I fall
and for putting me on the road again.
My heart's desire is to run with perseverance the race which
    you,
the Son of God,
have marked out for me.
Please help me to keep focused. Amen.

23: Peering Through the Pier

Hannah (four years) Jonathan (two years)

When our children were small, Frances took them with some friends to Clacton. In the afternoon they decided to go for a walk along the pier, to look at the view of the sea and coastline. The children, however, spent most of their time sprawled on their tummies looking through the tiny gaps between the planks of wood. They were intrigued by the glimpses of dark swirling water beneath the pier; much more interesting than gazing at the vast expanse of sea all around them. The sight of three children lying flat-out, squinting through the cracks was a funny one.

I learnt a lesson that day: As Frances and I reflected on the incident, it set us thinking about how we can become too limited in our outlook, especially if we only see things through the chink of our own experience. Our children would miss out on the vastness of the oceans and all the variety of colour and power contained within the sea if they spent *all* their time peering through the pier – if you know what I mean.

Perhaps it's a strange parallel to draw, but when I limit the work of God purely to my own ideals and expectations, a more complete experience of his love may well pass me by.

Of course, there's a time and a place for *'peering through the pier'* – just as Jesus took time to be focused in his life and ministry. Yet, if I'm honest, I feel that I sometimes need to broaden my horizons and enlarge my vision. For when

Christians stand up with their eyes open to the big wide world, they can become breathless and bowled over by the beauty and diversity of God's creation.

Bible Readings:

When I look . . .	Psalm 8
God has shown his kindness	Acts 14:8–17
Without excuse	Romans 1:18–25

A Prayer

Creator God,
I praise you for the beautiful world in which I live.
Forgive me for my lack of perspective and blinkered vision;
for the way in which I have lived selfishly and carelessly.
As I open my eyes to the glory of your creative handiwork,
may I also recognise all that has spoilt and abused it.
So let me gaze upon the wood of the Cross,
and through it see forgiveness and hope –
the possibility of glorious spiritual re-creation in my heart,
thanks to Jesus, the Saviour of the world. Amen.

24: Like a . . . Dinosaur?

Hannah (seven years)

One summer evening, after Hannah had returned from a holiday play scheme, she said to her mum, 'Have you seen the film Godzilla, Mummy?' 'No, I haven't,' came the intrigued reply. Then Hannah said, 'They were talking about it today. Is it about God?' 'Well, I see where you get the idea,' said Mum, 'but, actually, it's about a make-believe monster, like a dinosaur, called 'Godzilla'. 'Oh,' said Hannah, trying to please, 'I just thought it would've been good to see it if it was about God!'

I learnt a lesson that day: Things are not always as wholesome and appropriate as they may seem. Frances and I are keen *not* to wrap our children up in cotton wool. Nevertheless, we are concerned about the power of peer pressure – even at their tender age! I've not seen the film in question. It may be good, but is it appropriate for a seven-year-old? I can remember being petrified of Dr Who and the Yetis at a similar age. It gave me nightmares then, but now the re-runs of the series make me laugh.

It's great to see Hannah's earnest desire to find God in everything. As she gets older, this is something that requires discernment when she realises that life isn't always that simple and clear cut. I hope I'll always encourage my children to search for truth and goodness and to be able to distinguish between what is wholesome and what isn't. Furthermore, I want to influence them positively through my own example and prayers. For what applies to children also applies to me. I have to be aware of the peer pressure surrounding me and look to Jesus for guidance in deciding what's appropriate for *me* to watch. Jesus said: *'But when he, the Spirit of truth comes, he will guide you into all truth . . .' (John 16:13a)*

So, I mustn't be misled. The kingdom of God isn't 'like a dinosaur' – horrific and extinct. It's alive and present all around me, but revealed in love and purity.

Bible Readings:

The work of the Holy Spirit	John 16:5–16
Guide me in your truth	Psalm 25
Walking in the truth	2 and 3 John

A Prayer

God of truth,
I find this world confusing at times;
there are so many grey areas!
I want to walk in the truth,
but I do so need your guidance.
Fill me, I pray,
with your Spirit of truth,
that today I may keep my Christian integrity
and be protected from all that is evil and unhealthy.
I ask this in the name of Jesus,
whose precious blood can purify all sin. Amen.

25: Going Down

Hannah (eight years) Jonathan (six years)

How would you like to be in a high-speed elevator that shoots up thirteen storeys to the top of a building called *Terror Towers*? Once at the top, the doors open so that you can see the magnificent view. Doesn't sound *too* bad, does it? Yet, what if that lift then plummets like a stone, without warning and just before reaching the bottom returns at break-neck speed to the top again? What if all this is done in the dark with people screaming? Three times, in fact, before you are able to put your feet firmly on the ground again and escape!

Well, *Terror Towers* is one of the thrill rides at Disney World's MGM Studios and my children persuaded me to queue up and accompany them as they braved the foreboding challenge. I tried to deter them saying, '*I*,' sorry, '*they*, might be very frightened!' The children were confident, however, that they'd enjoy the ride.

They were right, of course, even though we were screaming – apart from Hannah, that is. We couldn't believe it. She had prepared herself and was calm and as quiet as a mouse throughout. This was quite a contrast to later on, when we sat down to eat and she unexpectedly fell off a low stool. The irony was that, following less than a two-foot drop, the tears flowed!

I learnt a lesson that day: When I know there are going to be difficult times ahead, I can prepare myself to face the challenges head on. Yet, on other occasions, it's the more minor trials that can take me by surprise and I find myself caught off guard. I can overreact and allow trivial things to become all out of proportion. Hannah's tears reminded me that God is with me in the ordinary moments, as well as the momentous. He can give the courage and peace that I need and help me to keep things in perspective. So, whatever terror towers over me each day, I need to say a prayer and prepare myself for all the challenging moments the day will bring.

Bible Readings:

Be strong and courageous	Joshua 1:1–9
Elijah makes a brave stand	1 Kings 18
Jesus sustained by the Holy Spirit	Luke 4:14–30

A Prayer

Sometimes Lord,
I feel that I just can't cope with life's challenges and surprises.
Yet, you are always with me
and can give the courage and peace that I need.
Help me never to be discouraged or terrified,
but to face the small and large hurdles of each day
in the power of your Spirit.
O Lord God Almighty, you are my strength and my protector.
  Amen.

26: From a Distance

Hannah (eight years) Jonathan (six years)

When we were in America, the Miles family witnessed the launch of the space shuttle 'Discovery' from the Kennedy Space Center. It was a spectacular sight, especially to see and hear the spacecraft as it disappeared from sight into the beautiful blue sky. As I looked up from a pier on Cocoa Beach, I was filled with a sense of awe and wonder at the display of technology and power. The children, however, took all this excitement in their stride, as if they had seen an ordinary jet take off from Gatwick. They were more interested in the dolphins swimming in the sea below us. No doubt one day they'll realise the significance of the occasion, even if the dolphins remain more memorable. Afterwards, Jonathan *did* ask lots of questions: 'Where is the shuttle now? Is it dark where the astronauts are? What can they see from out there?' And so on.

Back at home, a few weeks later, Jonathan was looking at the equator on his globe when he asked, 'Can *astronauts* see the red line round the middle of the world from space?'

I learnt a lesson that day: I pondered the spectacular views that the astronauts must have had from the shuttle – with the naked eye the world must look so peaceful and beautiful from a distance. Okay, the equator line couldn't be seen, but neither could the astronauts see all that's going on in the world: the wars and human suffering, the pollution, the traffic jams on the M25, the stress and the strife! Seeing Jonathan clutching his globe reminded me of the vastness of space and yet how small and insignificant the earth must have looked from out there. What's even more awesome is my belief that the all-powerful Creator God can see every human being in the world perfectly clearly and not *from a distance*. It's a sobering thought that just as I was monitoring the shuttle and its progress, my Creator was concerned about me and observing the way I live within his world. Though God may *seem* distant at times, I'm conscious that he is closer to me than my own heartbeat and is watching me attentively every day.

Bible Readings:

A God who is near	Jeremiah 23:23–24
Lord over the heavens, earth and sea	Isaiah 44:23–28
Worship to the Creator	Psalm 95

A Prayer

Maker of all,
when I open my eyes,
I am overwhelmed by the beauty of your creation.
You are a mighty God
and worthy of all honour and praise.
Alleluia!
It's amazing and I can't take it in,
for you are also like a gentle, caring parent,
who has known and loved me from when I was first formed in
    the womb.
Hold me in the hollow of your hand, I pray,
as I bow down in worship. Amen.

27: The Big Yawn

Hannah (eight years) Jonathan (six years)

How often have you heard the words, 'But it's boring!'? My children learnt them very quickly and I can even remember grumbling in the same vein when I was a teenager – just a few years ago *(cough)*. In this action-packed and thrill-seeking generation, the complaint of being *bored* seems to be even more prevalent, if not contagious. Even in Magic Kingdom, Florida, I heard Hannah utter, 'But it's boring!' She was moaning because one ride just wasn't as exciting as all the others. How can anyone be *bored* at Disney? If that's the case, what hope is there for the rest of life?

One day, having returned from America, we were getting ready to go to church. I don't need to tell you what Jonathan said. Now *he* might think that our church is boring, but as his dad *and* minister, I couldn't possibly comment! Yes, of course, as a leader of worship, I want services to be interesting, relevant, and Spirit led. However, they won't *always* be lively and entertaining. I have taken people to task for judging church services on a scale of 1–10 using such criteria. In the Bible it says there is: '. . . *a time to weep and a time to laugh, a time to mourn and a time to dance* . . .' *(Ecclesiastes 3:4)* There's a time and a season for everything.

I learnt a lesson that day: If I live life expecting every moment to be action packed, fun and wonderful, I'll surely be disappointed. Yes, Jesus came that I might have life in all its fullness *(John 10:10)*, but that doesn't mean it will always be entertaining, fulfilling, or simply what I want it to be! Children and adults alike have to learn that life has its ups and downs. We can feel on the top of the world, or down in the valleys, or simply on the level, but that's life! It's strange how God can powerfully use the ordinary or tough times. The question is: 'What do I make of *every* moment God gives me?' Sometimes I need to be less critical, more expectant and open to the Spirit of God. By the way, Hannah and Jonathan had a great time when they eventually got to their church, but I guess it would be really *boring* to point that out!

Bible Readings:

God of the hills, plains and valleys	1 Kings 20:22–29
Paul positive in prison	Philippians 1:1–21
Forget not his benefits	Psalm 103

A Prayer

Lord,
I'm so ungrateful!
Too often I want things all my own way.
Set me free from the chains of selfishness
and help my heart to rejoice,
despite my circumstances.
Guide me through the uncharted terrain of life,
that I may live every moment for you. Amen.

28: Thrills and Spills

Hannah (eight years) Jonathan (six years)

You can't admit to being a *chicken* if you're a daddy. My children have this habit of heading for the scariest rides when they visit a fairground or theme park. This manifested itself when, as a family, we visited Disney World, Florida. As a protective father, I quietly discounted the thrill rides on the guide map that had special warnings for expectant mothers, or for people with heart conditions. In no time at all however, Hannah and Jonathan managed to sniff out the most exciting and daring roller coasters in the park. As they laughed and giggled before each ride commenced, I was building up their confidence, but out of the corner of my eye I was also checking to see how secure it all looked, carefully noting any rusty nuts and bolts, while mentally convincing myself it must be safe or they wouldn't let the children on!

I guess, as I've got older, I've become more cautious and more aware. It's easier to worry and harder to trust. I almost felt guilty when I realised that the children's trust was more in me than it was in the ride itself. If Daddy was there, they'd be OK!

I learnt a lesson that day: I think God understands that grown-ups ask more questions about life and are prone to doubt and worry. They can easily become cynical and lose their optimism. Sometimes that's healthy, but there are times when I think God wants me to trust him simply and allow him to take me on an adventure of faith. He wants me to trust that others have been there before me and haven't been disappointed. There's a way to understand *faith* that I find helpful: **F.A.I.T.H.** which can stand for 'Forsaking All I Trust Him'. This *chicken* is good at asking questions, but perhaps I need to develop a deeper trust in my Heavenly Father, so that I may enjoy his 'ride-of-a-lifetime' with my children.

Bible Readings:

Faith	Hebrews 11:1–40
Abram and the promise	Genesis 15:1–6
A timid woman's faith	Luke 8:43–48

A Reflection

When we walk with the Lord
In the light of his word,
What a glory he sheds on our way!
While we do his good will,
He abides with us still,
And with all who will trust and obey:

Trust and obey, for there's no other way
To be happy in Jesus, but to trust and obey.

John Henry Sammis (1846–1919)

Lifted High

A little kid ran across the street
runny-nosed, a bit scruffy
tripping over almost.
She ran towards a man whose
arms were opened wide to
welcome her.
'Give us a swing Jesus,' she said,
and she felt herself lifted high
and she saw the street and the sky whirling
around her, ablaze with colour,
like a mixed-up rainbow.
She was laughing then –
excited, free
gasping for breath
'enough' she said
and she felt herself slowing down
relaxing, safe, as Jesus
held her in his arms
and smiled . . .

Unless we become like little children
Unless we risk that joy and abandonment
Unless we run and ask and let ourselves
be lifted high

We are never going to enter the Kingdom of God

© 1996 Kathy Galloway
'Lifted High' by Ruth Burgess from:
'The Pattern of our Days: Liturgies and Resources for Worship'
– Kathy Galloway (ed).
Published by Wild Goose Publications, Glasgow G2 3DH Scotland
Used with kind permission.

AT CHRISTMAS

'I'm going to be Joseph – I don't mind, as long as I don't have to kiss Mary.'

Jonathan Miles (five years)

29: Tummy Ache

Jonathan (four years)

Don't we say some silly things sometimes? Such as: 'The kettle's boiling!' You may have already said it today. The fact is, we don't actually mean the kettle's boiling; if it is, boy, we really are in trouble!

It often takes the questions of a young child to expose the weakness of some of our phrases, like the oft-quoted, 'I know how you feel'. One day, whilst out shopping, Jonathan said, 'Mum, I wish you were me and I was you.' Now, Frances wasn't quite sure what he was going to come out with next, but she hesitantly asked, 'Why?' Eventually the reply came: 'Because . . . if you was me, and I was you, then you'd know how much my tummy hurts!' If I were to say to Jonathan, 'I know how you feel,' he'd probably respond, 'Oh no you don't!' – and he'd be right.

I learnt a lesson that day: However sincerely I try, unless I've stood in another person's shoes, I can never tell if they're pinching. It's an important lesson to learn.

In which case, what about God? Can he ever tell how any human being feels? Well, I believe that God *has* taken a significant step to know how we feel. When Jesus was born, it was as though God *stepped into our shoes* and lived among us as a man. He didn't remain aloof from the problems of the world he created, but exposed himself to life as we know it – with all its joy and pain.

So, we don't have to wish that we were God and he were us. We simply have to remember and believe that God *is* with us and understands us – however we are feeling today!

Bible Readings:

God with us	Matthew 1:18–25
Jesus made in human likeness	Philippians 2:5–11
God knows us	Psalm 139

A Prayer

Ever loving God,
help me to trust that wherever I am,
however I'm feeling,
no matter what I'm going through,
you know and understand me completely.
Assure me of your presence
and grant me your help and guidance.
Make me mindful of the needs of others too,
through Jesus Christ our Lord. Amen.

30: Not a Shepherd!

Jonathan (four years)

After a nativity service, my son Jonathan was asked whether he enjoyed taking part. His reply was passionate: 'I didn't like wearing that green thing on my head. I didn't want to be a shepherd. I wanted to be a baddy, like a Power Ranger!'

Well, to my knowledge there aren't any Power Rangers in the Christmas story, so there's no wonder he didn't get the part. The problem was that walking on stage and standing still wasn't enough for my 'super-hero loving' boy.

I learnt a lesson that day: Understandably, our portrayal of the Christmas story can sometimes be very twee. Year after year, we're presented with a lovely familiar scene: Mary and Joseph beaming with contentment, even though they'd experienced a birth in the muck and mire. Baby Jesus asleep in the hay – some chance! Then there are the sweet, squeaky clean, mild mannered shepherds, gazing paternally at the snug little manger.

In reality we've been lulled by a tame version of events. It's no wonder children don't find it very exciting. The fact is, the nativity scene was profoundly *'down to earth'* and action packed: The shepherds would've been a rum lot of poor outcasts – ruddy working men, who fearfully responded and obediently made their way to Bethlehem. They then saw the newly born Son of God in a smelly stable! Born in humility, rather than showing the *range* of God's *power*.

Afterwards, these ordinary shepherds went on their way rejoicing and telling people about the extraordinary thing they had seen. People were amazed at what they heard, probably because it was all so strange. What a night that must've been and how important those shepherds were!

One day, I'll explain to Jonathan that there's more to being a shepherd than wearing a tea towel on your head. It has to do with being a true man and responding to Jesus – a real 'super-hero' – if ever there was one!

Bible Readings:

The shepherds and the angels   Luke 2:8–20
The greatest Shepherd of them all   John 10:1–18
A promised ruler from Bethlehem   Micah 5:1–5

A Prayer

Holy Child of Bethlehem,
at your birth ordinary shepherds were drawn
to kneel before your throne of wood and straw.
Receive my worship, I pray,
and help me to live honestly in the real world.
I rejoice in you Christ Jesus!
Help me to share the Good News with others. Amen.

31: God and Ladders

Jonathan (four years)

On his way home from the shops, my son saw a long ladder leaning against one of the houses down our road. There was no one climbing it; the decorators were probably taking one of their numerous 'tea breaks'. It was, therefore, strange that a ladder should captivate Jonathan's attention for so long. Eventually, he said dreamily, 'I wish . . . I wish there was a special clip on every ladder in the world, so that they could all be joined together and I could climb up and see God . . . and Jesus!'

What a lovely picture. For generations people have wondered about heaven. Where is it? Where's God and what does he look like? I don't think we ever lose that insatiable child-like curiosity; our questions just get more complicated. Yet, if we're not careful, we can run out of energy and tie ourselves in theological knots trying to comprehend the great mysteries of God.

I learnt a lesson that day: It's good to explore deeply profound questions, but perhaps we're not meant to be climbing up to find God, in order to see what he looks like. I've learnt that we can't make our own way to him. The great Christian truth is that in love he comes to us. Yes, in Jesus, God invested himself in his creation in the lowly form of a baby, born in Bethlehem. Those who came to see the Holy Child had to look down with humility into a manger and not up into the heavens.

The trouble is, it's tempting to *climb the ladders* of this world and struggle to reach new heights of success, goodness, wisdom, power and the like. Maybe I ought to bend my knee a little more and fix my eyes on Jesus. Surely that's the way for Jonathan and me to behold God in all his glory!

Bible Readings:

Bow down and worship	Matthew 2:1–12
Jacob's dream at Bethel	Genesis 28:10–22
Ambition	Mark 10:35–45

A Prayer

Gracious God,
thank you for taking the initiative to find me
and making it possible for me to discover you,
through Jesus Christ, my Saviour.
May I bow down and worship you as the One who is very near
and seek to serve you here on earth,
just as Jesus came to serve
and give his life as a ransom for many.
In his name, I pray. Amen.

32: Making a Point

Hannah (seven years)

Following an exhausting day at school, Hannah, who was in year three at the time, was chatting enthusiastically about her day. In the midst of this she said, 'You know it's rude to point at people. Well, when I put my hand up in class to answer a question, I try to keep my fingers down . . . so that I'm not pointing at God!'

I had to admire her sensitivity, but felt I should explain to her teacher why my daughter had a limp wrist. Of course, she was right. It *is* rude to point an accusing finger. Putting your hand up at school, however, is hardly the same thing. There *are* occasions when it's quite appropriate to point.

I learnt a lesson that day: The season of Advent is a time when we prepare for Christmas. In the Bible we see the prophets pointing to the coming of a Messiah. We also see John the Baptist preparing the way for the Lord: when he saw Jesus he said, *'Look, the Lamb of God, who takes away the sin of the world!'* (John 1:29b)

As a Christian, I feel I ought to be pointing to Jesus at Christmas; not in a rude way, but in my words and conduct, rather like someone who knows the answer to a question and enthusiastically wants to share it with others. Perhaps I can point to Jesus in practical ways; like inviting family, friends and neighbours to Christmas services; or by putting love into action and giving the glory to God, rather than accepting any praise for myself.

When Hannah knows the answer to a question at school, she looks as though she'll explode if she doesn't point out the answer to someone. May I learn from her example – with hands lifted high!

Bible Readings:

John points the way	John 1:29–36
Isaiah points to the Suffering Servant	Isaiah 52:13–53:12
Peter acknowledges Christ	Mark 8:27–38

A Prayer

Father,
help me to name the name of Jesus,
that others may know the reason for the faith that is in me,
for the sake of your kingdom. Amen.

33: Greetings

Hannah (seven years) Jonathan (five years)

The Christmas season brings plenty of excitement to the Miles household, especially when the postman staggers up the drive. The receiving of cards and news from family and friends is interesting and fun – all part of the festive chaos! This tradition began in Britain soon after the first Penny Post public delivery. I read that a thousand copies of the first commercial card were sold in London back in 1843. Now there are over two billion cards and letters posted each year.

One day my children were sitting in the lounge, each with a small table in front of them. They had a pile of cards and pens at the ready. Both Hannah and Jonathan dutifully went through their list of school friends. They then wrote cards to each other. When the last two were finished, they were quickly passed across the table and, within seconds, were opened and they thanked each other. It was all very sweet and there was peace and goodwill in the home! Then, all of a sudden, the same little angels were squabbling over the one remaining card that was found left unused on the table.

I learnt a lesson that day: The practice of sending Christmas cards can, if I'm not careful, get out of hand and lose all meaning. The intended sentiments can easily become forgotten. Perhaps I should question the number of cards I post, the reason why I send them, or the amount of thought that goes into writing them. Then there's the issue as to whether or not I should give cards to people I see all the time. What about the words and the sentiments they convey? What's the message I really *should be* communicating? Am I being a good steward of the earth's resources? And finally, could the money I spend on paper, card and postage be used more carefully and wisely?

It's easy to forget the reason for the season when I write my cards. It's far harder to embody the message of Christmas and to allow it to really change my life and relationships. I reckon God knew what he was doing when he sent his Son, Jesus, and not a card for Christmas!

Bible Readings:

The reason	John 3:16–17
Simeon's knowledge	Luke 2:25–35
Love incarnate	1 John 4:8–16

A Prayer

To buy a card can be the easy way out and cheap.
Father, help me to give of myself and of my time.
My eyes have been opened to see your costly and precious gift of Jesus.
Open my heart and possess me with your Spirit,
so that your love may be made complete in my relationships.
Amen.

34: Not to be Missed

Jonathan (five years)

I really enjoy infant school Nativity plays. On one occasion
Jonathan was playing the part of a wise man. Just before he
came on stage there was the scene with the shepherds
making their way to the stable. I couldn't help but smile at
one of the little shepherds who, following the appearance
of the heavenly host, said, 'Come *(sigh)* let us see this thing
(sigh) that has happened.' He said it as though he'd been
there a thousand times and was now getting a bit fed up
with the story line – the baby in the manger was hardly a
surprise to him!

I learnt a lesson that day: If I let the Christmas story
become too familiar, there's a danger that the loveliness of
the traditional tale can lull me into a feeling that I've heard
it all before. The scene can almost become like a fairy story.

Now, at the time when Jonathan was in his Nativity play,
I hadn't yet seen the newly released film, Titanic. People
had told me it was excellent, but due to the busyness of life,
I'd been tempted to say, 'Why bother going to see a film
when you know what's going to happen anyway!' I knew
the beginning and the end. Could I afford three hours from
my schedule to go and view it? Of course, those who'd seen
it said, 'You don't know what you're missing, it's a moving
love story! What's more, unless you see it more than once,
you'll fail to spot things that are often overlooked the first
time around.'

I think there's a parallel here with the account of Jesus'

birth. It's easy to assume that I know the plot and so fail to experience new insights, or allow myself to be moved by this rich love story. I hope that I never get tired of Christmas. I've learnt that there's more to it than memories of enduring Nativity rehearsals with a tea towel on my head. I may have grown up, but a *wise* man never stops seeking. This, in itself, is a gift I can offer to Jesus.

Bible Readings:

Paul re-tells the familiar story	Romans 1:1–7
Mary responds to the greatest news	Luke 1:46–55
A teacher seeks the truth	John 3:1–21

A Prayer

God of the familiar and the unfamiliar;
God of the manger and the cross;
God of resurrection and hope;
refresh my understanding and speak to me anew.
Let my spirit rejoice in my Lord and Saviour
and in humility may I be set apart for the gospel. Amen.

35: ABC . . .

Hannah (six years) Jonathan (four years)

I like to listen to the radio when I'm in the car, but there have been times when it's been virtually impossible when my children were with me. Why? Well, the endless repetition of their cassettes was the only thing that kept them amused on a journey. The dreaded 'ABC . . .' tape was my least favourite. It was a really hypnotic Christmas present that, if you weren't careful, could literally drive you up the wall.

The twenty-six letters were sung over and over and over again, helping absorbent little minds to learn the alphabet. Hannah and Jonathan loved singing along – much to the amusement of those who overtook us! It may have been monotonous and really annoying but, as I thought about it, I was reminded that the alphabet is vitally important. It's a tool that unlocks a new world!

I learnt a lesson that day: These twenty-six letters have been used by authors to enthral us with mysteries and to move us with love stories; by entertainers to raise our spirits with humour and song; by teachers to educate and challenge us with wisdom and insight; by rulers and governments to issue decrees. Parents have used letters, formed into words, to guide children who, in turn, have used them to inspire and delight adults.

Words were spoken powerfully by Jesus, telling us how we should live and revealing God's love. In fact, Jesus likened himself to the beginning and end of the Greek alphabet: *'I am the Alpha and the Omega,'* he said. *(Revelation 1:8a)* In Jesus, we find completeness. He is the key to unlocking the meaning of life and to being 'born again' to a new world of discovery. No wonder St John spoke of the Word becoming flesh when referring to Jesus. *(John 1:14a)* Perhaps I should pay attention to the way I use the precious gift of words. For the sake of *the Word* – the gift of God for me.

Bible Readings:

| The Word became flesh | John 1:1–14 |
| Alpha and Omega | Revelation 1:8; 21:5–7; and 22:13 |

A Prayer

Eternal God,
thank you for the gift of language;
help me to use words lovingly and creatively.
Just as you have expressed yourself clearly in Jesus,
may I be transformed by your Holy Spirit,
to receive, embody and impart your words
that are trustworthy and true. Amen.

Child of the Stable's Secret Birth

Child of the stable's secret birth,
the Lord by right of the lords of earth,
let angels sing of a King new-born,
the world is weaving a crown of thorn:
a crown of thorn for that infant head
cradled soft in the manger bed.

Eyes that shine in the lantern's ray;
a face so small in its nest of hay,
face of a child who is born to scan
the world he made through the eyes of man:
and from that face in the final day
earth and heaven shall flee away.

Voice that rang through the courts on high
contracted now to a wordless cry,
a voice to master the wind and wave,
the human heart and the hungry grave:
the voice of God through the cedar trees
rolling forth as the sound of seas.

Infant hands in a mother's hand,
for none but Mary may understand
whose are the hands and the fingers curled
but his who fashioned and made our world;
and through these hands in the hour of death
nails shall strike to the wood beneath.

Child of the stable's secret birth,
the Father's gift to a wayward earth,
to drain the cup in a few short years
of all our sorrows, our sins and tears;
ours the prize for the road he trod:
risen with Christ; at peace with God.

AT PLAY

Gentle Jesus, meek and mild,
Look upon a little child,
Pity my simplicity,
Suffer me to come to thee.

(*Charles Wesley 1707–1788*)

36: On the Ball

Jonathan (five years)

Scotland were playing Brazil in the first round of the World Cup. Jonathan was watching intently and making all sorts of helpful comments, like: 'Which way *are* Scotland supposed to be kicking Daddy?'

Well, the game and atmosphere got even more exciting and Mum and Dad were glued to the TV. At a crucial moment, Jonathan enquired casually, 'But why do we have football anyway?' What a moment to pose such a profound question. Nevertheless, I guess it would've won the sympathy of those who were finding the World Cup boring. Jonathan was far from bored, so I was amazed that in the midst of the excitement he could step back from the action and ask such a thought-provoking question.

I learnt a lesson that day: Am I able to step back a bit from the hurly-burly of daily living and ask a few *why* questions for myself? Do I consider why I've been given the gift of life? What is it for? Why do I do what I do? The fact is, in my busyness, it's easy to let such questions pass by. Yet, unless I wrestle with them, there's no hope of beginning to discover the answers. You see, I think *football* is different from *life*, as such. It can be enjoyed fully without needing to know why the game exists. *Life*, however, can have greater meaning and purpose if I take time out to explore a few fundamental *why* questions. I'm more likely to discover the goal my Creator intends me to aim for.

By the way, I think I know why football was invented in

the first place. Apparently, it was something to do with keeping young men away from distractions of the feminine variety. But, for a little boy, I'll have to come up with a better answer than that!

Bible Readings:

Job begins to ask, why?	Job 3
Habakkuk asks, why?	Habakkuk 1:1–3:19
Why worry?	Luke 12:13–34

A Prayer

I busy myself with 'How?', 'What?', 'When?' and 'Where?'
But why don't I make more time to ask 'Why?' and 'Who?',
*   Lord?*
Help me to reflect today
and consider the meaning and purpose of life,
for the sake of Jesus Christ my Lord. Amen.

37: Team Work

Jonathan (five years)

Jonathan finds numbers interesting and he's also football mad. Shortly before his sixth birthday he declared: 'If . . . if there were 4,168 girls and just me and Joe, then us boys would thrash those girls at football, because we're brilliant!'

Now far be it from me to encourage a battle of the sexes (he has a few lessons to learn in that respect) but it's good to see Jonathan has confidence in himself; a sense of self-worth and a recognition of his gifts.

I learnt a lesson that day: I should never be tempted to believe I have nothing to offer and I'm not worth anything. It's easy to think I'm too young or too old; not talented or bright enough to be used by God. At his tender age, Jonathan is secure enough to believe he has something to offer – even football!

I'm reminded of a familiar story from the Bible, when a young boy simply has the confidence to give Jesus his packed lunch. What he offers the Lord is miraculously able to feed 5,000 people. Now that's a number that would really impress Jonathan!

So I need to remember, that if I give to God all that I am and all that I have, then I really will be on the winning side. What's more, I should keep playing football with my son and encourage and help him to develop his skills. Who knows, though he and Joe may never get the chance to take on 4,168 girls, they just might become key players in a successful team of 11.

Postscript: Three years after this, both Jonathan and Joe were signed up for Premiership academy teams!

Bible Readings:

A boy gives his lunch to Jesus	John 6:1–13
A boy called for a special purpose	1 Samuel 3:1–21
Parable of the ten minas	Luke 19:12–27

A Prayer

Take my life, and let it be
Consecrated, Lord, to thee;
Take my moments and my days,
Let them flow in ceaseless praise.

Take my hands, and let them move
At the impulse of thy love;
Take my feet, and let them be
Swift and beautiful for thee.

Frances Ridley Havergal (1836–1879)

38: Just a Minute

Jonathan (five years)

Table football used to be a favourite occupation for Jonathan. I have to say, he was brilliant. Well, he must have been, if he could beat me virtually every time. On a typically busy morning, the Miles family was trying to get ready for school. Unfortunately, I'd added to the pressure by promising Jonathan a game of football. It was a bad move. I only agreed because I'd suffered a crushing defeat the night before: 10–3, to be precise!

'Pleeease Dad! Please can I have that game now?' 'Oh OK,' I replied, 'I'll be with you in a minute.' The next thing I heard was a little boy walking up the stairs counting: '1, 2, 3, 4, 5 . . .' Then later, little feet coming down again: '57, 58, 59, . . . Dad, your minute's up! Football?' Again, I replied: 'Darling, I've got lots to do. In a minute!' Off he went again: '1, 2, 3, 4 . . .' Meanwhile, Mum explained to him that when grown-ups say 'in a minute', they don't always mean it literally. What they're really saying is 'fairly soon'. Jonathan replied, 'Well how much do I have to count up to for 'fairly soon?'' Frances smiled, but had no answer.

I learnt a lesson that day: I believe my Heavenly Father always keeps his promises and is faithful. His love is constant and he never lets me down. What's more, he's never too busy for me – as long as I turn to him in trust. Having said that, I need to examine his promises in the Bible carefully and be sure of their meaning. As I was taught at theological college: 'a *text* without a *context* is a *pre-text*.' It's worth pondering that one.

By the way, we did squeeze in another game of football and I lost yet again. I suppose it serves me right really. I certainly couldn't appeal for extra time, could I!

Bible Readings:

Jesus has a lot to do	Luke 4:38–44
God is faithful in all he does	Psalm 33
The Law and the promise	Galatians 3:15–25

A Prayer

Lord,
you are faithful and never too busy.
Your word is right and true
and your plans stand firm forever.
Help me to understand what you are saying to me,
so that I may graciously say what I mean
and mean what I say.
For I want to keep my promises to you and others,
as I walk in the freedom of faith all my days. Amen.

39: Rain Stopped Play

Jonathan (five years)

The weather always manages to find its way into conversation. Listeners to *Miles in the Morning* on Premier Christian Radio will know I often get calls asking me to be more positive when I give the weather forecast – even when the outlook's a bit gloomy! People remind me that this is the day that the Lord has made and I should rejoice and be glad in it! Well, I'd like to be more positive sometimes, but one definition of a *pessimist* is 'an *optimist* with all the facts'.

Those who like an optimistic slant to the weather would have been proud of Jonathan. When trying to persuade his mum to let him play football in the garden, he said: 'It's not raining, it's just pouring a little bit.'

On another occasion, in the middle of a terrific storm, Jonathan was trying to be brave. He said, 'Please God, make it thunder again, so that I can cuddle my mummy.' He'd recognised that he couldn't prevent the storm from taking place. Instead, all he could do was to acknowledge the source, let the storm happen and seek refuge.

I learnt a lesson that day: I may grumble about the weather but, at the end of the day, I need to accept that there are some things that are out of my control. This can be a hard lesson to learn. There are many things in my life that I do have control over. Nevertheless, however clever and resourceful I may, or may not be, the weather will always evoke within me a sense of awe, wonder and reverence before an Almighty Creator God.

When the storms of life come my way and things seem to be out of my control, I'd do well to turn and trust God. After all, he is the one who is my refuge and strength. Perhaps I should be more positive about that truth in daily conversation – whatever the weather!

Bible Readings:

Paul caught up in a storm	Acts 27:13–25
Jonah saved by a great fish	Jonah 1:1–17
The winds and waves obey Jesus	Luke 8:22–25

A Reflection

Be still, and know that I am God . . .

Psalm 46:10a

We have an anchor that keeps the soul
Steadfast and sure while the billows roll;
Fastened to the Rock which cannot move,
Grounded firm and deep in the Saviour's love!

Priscilla Owens (1829–1899)

40: 'But I Only Wanted Football!'

Hannah (seven years) Jonathan (five years)

Hannah had been given some lovely *hand-me-down* clothes from a family in our church. Receiving a bag of surprises from a trendy teenager was a real treat for her. She was delighted and took great pleasure in unpacking the clothing. She laid each item on the floor and then tried them on for size – one at a time. Jonathan had witnessed all this and was well aware of the happiness this had brought his sister. Hannah left the room, leaving a forlorn looking Jonathan on the sofa with his Mother. There was a silence followed by a very sorrowful, 'Mum, why can't . . .? Oh why can't I . . .?' Then Mum interrupted: 'Unfortunately, there's no-one to pass on boys' clothes to us at the moment, Jonathan.' Trying to smooth things over she continued, 'Most of our friends have got younger brothers or cousins, so they don't have any clothes to pass on to you, I'm afraid.' Jonathan was puzzled, not knowing what his mum was on about. 'No, Mum!' he said with a frown, 'Oh, why can't I go outside and play football?'

Frances and I thought it was funny that she'd totally misread the situation and had jumped to the wrong conclusion, assuming Jonathan was jealous of his sister.

I learnt a lesson that day: It's dangerous to make assumptions and to think that we know what another person is thinking – especially a child! How often do I butt in to someone's conversation, cutting them off in their prime, or finishing off a sentence for them? I'm glad God listens to me and patiently waits for me to tell him all my needs and sorrows, my hopes and fears. I believe he rarely interrupts and never misreads the situation.

I'm grateful for the generosity of friends, expressed through the gift of clothes. They brought much joy to a little girl and a gracious response from a young boy. Next time we'll let him finish what he's . . .

Bible Readings:

Be quick to listen	James 1:19–27
An outcast is given full attention	John 4:1–42
Listen to God	Proverbs 8:32–35

'God knew what he was doing when he gave us two ears and only one mouth.' *Anonymous*

A Prayer

God of the Word and the listening ear,
help me to control my tongue today
and to watch and wait for your prompting,
through your Holy Sprit. Amen.

41: Fast Forward

Jonathan (five years)

It was nearly Jonathan's sixth birthday, so as you can imagine, there was a lot of excitement in the Miles household. To top it all, football crazy Jonathan was elated when he heard the headlines at the time: England had beaten Poland at Wembley! His eyes were glued to the TV during the early evening news, and he was eagerly awaiting the live sports report – hoping to catch some highlights from the match. The trouble was that at that time, the war in Kosovo was understandably dominating the broadcast. After a while, Jonathan wearily said to his mum: 'Can't you fast forward this bit onto the football?' He didn't want to hear any more bad news about fighting and refugees; he was impatient and naturally wanted to focus on the good news: the triumph at Wembley! At his age, who could blame him? Obviously a little boy wasn't going to understand fully the seriousness of a war situation and why the England match was less highly rated.

I learnt a lesson that day: It can be tempting during Holy Week to want to *fast forward* to the Easter Day celebrations, without first dwelling on the events that led up to the triumph of Jesus' resurrection. Just as Jonathan needed to learn that life isn't always easy, or full of excitement, so I believe I need to consider the *whole* Easter story, including the more difficult and disturbing parts. Jesus' death was necessary and it's important that I face it. The glory of Easter Day can only be fully appreciated if I first understand Jesus' suffering love: his sacrifice for a broken and sinful world. Jesus didn't *fast forward* over the pain of his cruel death. Rather he demonstrated the extent of his love. It's because of this I can know he's present with me through the tough times. He understands and holds out the hope that ultimately I can share his victory and be part of his winning team of love!

Bible Readings:

Jesus foretells his suffering	Mark 10:32–34
Good Friday	Matthew 27:11–44
Job's anguish in suffering	Job 6:1–30

A Prayer

Then let us stand beneath the cross,
And feel his love a healing stream,
All things for him account but loss,
And give up all our hearts to him;
Of nothing think or speak beside:
My Lord, my Love is crucified.

Charles Wesley (1707–1788) alt.

42: The Lord's Side

Jonathan (six years)

As a special treat to celebrate his sixth birthday, I took Jonathan to his first football match. We went to see our local club Leyton Orient play West Ham. My son seemed very grown up as we sat on the train making our way to the game, but once in the stadium he looked so small and I became all protective. Occasionally, I had to cover his ears to shield him from words I'd rather he didn't hear. I also had to cover his mouth when he was shouting for the 'O's', whilst surrounded by supporters of the 'Hammers'. Fortunately they seemed to think it was funny. Throughout it all, he was blissfully unaware, caught up in the match with eyes wide open and a grin on his face – even though by half-time Orient were being thrashed 3–0!

Pondering the score, Jonathan turned to me and said, 'Dad, is it alright if I change sides and support West Ham now?' 'Of course you can't,' I said, even though I sympathised. 'Good supporters stay loyal to their team and don't change just because they're losing!' I'm not sure he was convinced, but he followed my advice and braved a 4–0 defeat with great dignity.

I learnt a lesson that day: It's tempting to follow the crowd when the going gets tough; to ally ourselves with strength, power and fame. If I'm honest, there are times when I compromise my ideals and find myself going with the flow of those around me. As I thought about Jonathan's words, I felt Jesus saying, 'Come and follow me.' He never promised his disciples an easy ride. At times it seemed as though his way was weak and could never deliver a result. Yet, I believe his team becomes stronger as more people give him their allegiance and keep following him through thick and thin. Moreover, if I let the Lord down, *he* never gives up on me. He simply reinstates me when I'm truly sorry, challenges me and is pleased when I remain loyal. I'm glad to be on the side of 'Followers United!'

Bible Readings:

Against a mighty warrior	1 Samuel 17
Who is the greatest?	Mark 9:33–37
Be strong and endure hardship	2 Timothy 2:1–13

A Prayer

God my defender,
it's hard to be a Christian when others accuse me of being weak
and it appears that I'm a loser in this ambitious world.
Help me to remember that if I want to be first in your kingdom,
I must be the very last and the servant of all.
Then I shall be strong in the grace that is in Christ Jesus.
May I follow the Lord as part of the triumphant fellowship of
*   the faithful. Amen.*

A Child's View of Heaven: The Door

There was once a very large door, hidden away in the left hand corner of the room.

One day a young girl looked through the keyhole and saw a small room containing a set of Barbie dolls.

One day a car mechanic looked through the keyhole and saw all the cars fixed.

One day an author looked through the keyhole and saw his books selling to millions.

One day a poor man looked through the keyhole and saw him being rich.

One day an orphan looked through the keyhole and saw a loving family.

One day a sad boy looked the keyhole and saw happiness.

One day a footballer looked through the keyhole and saw him being man of the match.

One day a ghost looked through the keyhole and saw his flesh and blood.

One day a policeman looked through the keyhole and saw his promotion badge.

One day a dog looked through the keyhole and saw a juicy bone.

One day a soldier looked through the keyhole and saw peace.

One day a homeless man looked through the keyhole and saw a new life.

One day a baby looked through the keyhole and saw himself as a man.

One day a nurse looked through the keyhole and saw all her patients well.

One day the door opened and inside was Heaven.

By William Wright (11 years)
© William Wright 2000. Used with kind permission.

AT THE TABLE

'How sharper than a serpent's tooth it is
To have a thankless child!'

William Shakespeare (1564–1616) – King Lear

43: 'Wot, No Grace?'

Hannah (three years)

The time had come for me, as a minister, to move to a new church appointment. Part of this process involves being interviewed by stewards from churches with a forthcoming vacancy. Of course, such a move is bathed in prayer, but nonetheless, it's a nerve-racking experience. Just as with any kind of career interview, you want to show yourself in the right light and ensure you give of your very best.

On one occasion, I can remember being very interested in a prospective appointment and felt it was where God wanted me to be. My wife and elder child were with me and we were sitting down with the circuit steward to enjoy the meal set before us. 'Please do start,' came the instruction. Without hesitation I obediently raised a piece of quiche to my lips. Instantly, my daughter, Hannah, said, 'But aren't we going to say *Grace*?' I don't know who was more embarrassed, me or the steward concerned. 'Quite right, Hannah!' said the host, 'fancy forgetting.' He promptly invited me to say a prayer – when I'd finished my mouthful!

This reminded me of an occasion when I was preaching in the Welsh valleys. A family had kindly provided Sunday lunch. Before we ate the father said, 'Let's say *Grace*.' Immediately his son retorted, 'Why Dad? We don't normally!' Don't you just love the blatant honesty of children? Well, going back to my interview, it went well and I was very proud of my daughter.

I learnt a lesson that day: I must be careful not to get so caught up in what I'm doing, however important it may be, that I forget to say thank you to God for his love and provision. I believe the tradition of saying thank you to him in prayer before a meal is not only good training for children, but also a worthy discipline for everyone. It draws people closer to each other and to God himself. Furthermore, it provides a valuable pause for thought, which I'm sure pleases our Creator. Why not give *Grace* a try today – or else Hannah might be after you!

Bible Readings:

Jesus gives thanks	Mark 6:30–44
Jesus and another meal	1 Corinthians 11:23–26
Thanksgiving for God's loving care	Deuteronomy 26:1–11

A Prayer

Faithful God,
forgive me for failing to acknowledge all I take for granted
    everyday:
a plentiful supply of food, running water and shelter too.
Help me never to forget those who live in poverty
and don't even know where their next meal is coming from.
For Jesu's sake, help me to share what I have with others. Amen.

44: The Wide World

Hannah (five years) Jonathan (three years)

It was teatime and everything was ready to be served. We were taking our place at the table just as fish fingers, mashed potatoes and peas were being dished up. My son opened his eyes in delight and spontaneously said, 'Mummy, you're the best cook in the *wide world.*' His sister, Hannah, replied with all the wisdom of a five-year-old, 'No, Jonathan, it's supposed to be God, isn't it?'

Well, on this occasion, Mum didn't mind being relegated to second position. We giggled, imagining God as 'Divine Gourmet'.

Later that day, and for no particular reason, Jonathan exercised his new-found phrase: 'You're the best, Dad, and I love you in the *wide world.*' I treasure moments like these and hold on to them when he's not being such a little angel.

I learnt a lesson that day: It's so important to encourage people and to express love. Frequently, I'm guilty of taking people for granted. I forget to offer words of appreciation and acknowledgement, especially when they're not expected. I spend time teaching my children to say 'thank you' and yet there are times when I'm just as slow to learn.

It made me wonder how God my Heavenly Father feels. He must take great delight when his children really open their eyes wide and appreciate his creation and goodness; when they turn to him and say, 'Abba, Father, you're the best and I love you in the *whole wide world.*'

Bible Readings:

An expression of loving praise	Psalm 145
Practical instructions	1 Thessalonians 5:11–28
The importance of thankfulness	Luke 17:11–19

A Prayer

Heavenly Father,
I'm sorry for taking you for granted.
Forgive me!
I have failed to express my love and gratitude
in response to all that you are
and all you have given.
I thank you for expressing your love and encouragement.
May your Holy Spirit enable me to reflect your nature,
that others may know the wonder of your love
and be inspired to worship and adore you,
through Jesus Christ, our Lord. Amen.

45: Think of a Number

Hannah (six years) Jonathan (four years)

It all started after school as we were sitting round the tea table. Frances and I were encouraging Hannah to recite her ten times table. We explained to her and Jonathan that it was really important to learn the tables by heart, saying: 'Mum and Dad had to learn them when they were at school and, though it was hard work, it was definitely worth it. Now we don't have to think too long when we do our sums in shops, for example.' (Well, most of the time!) Before Hannah could suggest the use of a calculator, we all started practising: one ten is 10, two tens are 20, three tens are 30 . . . twelve tens are 120! We all thought we'd done well and a confidence came over Hannah as she tried her 100 times table! There was a pause and then she said: 'What's a hundred times 100? Is that the last number?' We began to explain that numbers go on into infinity, so we don't know what the last number is – they're never ending. No-one knows! Hannah then replied, 'I expect Jesus knows the last number!'

I learnt a lesson that day: Hannah had such certainty that her Lord would know the answer to a question that nobody else would know. It challenged me about my own ability to trust Jesus when I reach the limit of my own understanding. There are some things that I'll never know and perhaps I'm not meant to know – especially about the future. The second verse of a hymn came to mind:

'Tis Jesus, the first and the last, whose spirit shall guide us safe home; We'll praise him for all that is past, and trust him for all that's to come.'

(Joseph Hart 1712–1768)

Yes, I'm sure Jesus does know the last number – whatever it is! Anyway, back to the art of multiplication that every disciple needs to learn. After all, Jesus told Peter that we should forgive people, not seven times, but seventy times seven. Don't feel bad if you can't work it out – it's just a lot!

Bible Readings:

The unmerciful servant	Matthew 18:21–35
Some things we don't know	Matthew 24:36–44
Trust in God, not numbers	Judges 7

A Prayer

God of infinity,
there is no end to you.
You are love without limit;
unfathomable grace;
inexhaustible hope!
As you were with me from the beginning,
remain with me always, I pray. Amen.

46: 'Bon Appetit!'

Hannah (six years) Jonathan (four years)

On one of my many parental taxi runs, I went to pick up Jonathan who had been to a friend's house for tea. Andrew was his class mate and they were both nearly five years old. I discovered that they'd had a whale of a time playing together.

On arrival, I was met by Andrew's mum (who's French). With a smile she told me what happened when she sat the boys down to eat. Apparently, she put a question to Jonathan: 'Do you know what people in France say just before their meal?' The expected reply was: 'Bon appetit.' My son, however, said very matter of factly, 'Grace in French?' That's my boy! 'What would you expect from the son of a minister?' Andrew's mum said in her beautiful French accent. Mais oui!

I learnt a lesson that day: It made no difference to Jonathan that a person spoke differently. 'Grace' was still the right thing to say before a meal – a thank you to God. It reminded me of a holiday in France, when Hannah asked, 'Does God speak French or English?' Of course the answer was *both* and *more*, because, believe it or not, God's not English. I want my children to grow up knowing that their Heavenly Father loves *all* people in the world equally: language, culture or colour makes absolutely no difference!

I believe God's heart is broken where there are people who are not able to enjoy all the food that we do. So, if you've tucked into coffee and croissants this morning, or even a full English breakfast, ask yourself, 'Did I pause to remember those who are less fortunate? Did I pray for them? Am I thankful for all I have?' It's good practice wherever you are. True gratitude can bring about change in poorer countries through generous hearts – in places where they'd love to be able to say Grace and 'Bon appetit!'

Bible Readings:

Giving and receiving	Philippians 4:10–20
All one in Christ	Galatians 3:26–29
Feast of Weeks and Tabernacles	Deuteronomy 16:9–17

A Prayer

When I live life at a pace
and fail to say Grace,
I am selfish and greedy
and forget those who are needy.
So, let me say, 'Thank you!' today
and remember to pray
to the One who graciously feeds me. Amen.

47: Pause for Thought

Hannah (seven years) Jonathan (five years)

In the Miles household, however hungry we are, we try to remember to say Grace before our main meal. We take it in turns to say a simple prayer of thanksgiving to God. Sometimes the children's prayers can cause a smile. Hannah once prayed: 'Thank you for our food! . . . If we didn't have food we would die and you *would* be upset, God. Amen.' On another occasion, Jonathan raised an eyebrow with the words, 'Dear God, we *hope* we have a nice meal today!' Well, I understood what he meant, but Mum wasn't so sure!

Being younger than his sister, Jonathan sometimes couldn't think what to say when it was his turn to say Grace. On such occasions he would lapse into a prayer he learnt by heart: *'Bless our school, that in working together and playing together we may learn to serve you and love one another!'* Hannah took a dim view of this, saying: 'But Jonathan, that's not a Grace, because you haven't said thank you for our food.'

I learnt a lesson that day: In one sense Hannah was quite right. Nevertheless, even as an adult there are times when I struggle to find the appropriate words to pray. So often I fall back on familiar prayers, Bible verses, hymns or worship songs. Somehow they become an inner resource – words that spring immediately to mind. It would seem the same thing happened to Jesus: time after time he quoted verses by heart; words he'd learnt probably as a child.

Perhaps that's why he gave us the Lord's Prayer to learn. He knew it could help us when we just can't find the words. To use a well-worn prayer is better than *not* praying at all. Thanks to God, I find the more I pause for thought, the easier and more appropriate my prayer becomes. What amazing grace!

Bible Readings:

Jesus teaches his disciples to pray	Luke 11:1–4
The Psalmist delights in God's law	Psalm 119:9–16
The New Covenant	Jeremiah 31:31–34

A Prayer

For all thy gifts we bless thee, Lord,
But chiefly for our heavenly food,
Thy pardoning grace, thy quickening word,
These prompt our song, that God is good.

John Hampden Gurney (1802–1862)

48: 'Why Are They There?

Hannah (six years) Jonathan (four years)

It was a cold wet day in London and the Miles family was seeking a restaurant for warmth and food. All of a sudden, Hannah saw three homeless men wrapped in sleeping bags and sheltering from the weather. Sadly this is not an uncommon sight, but new to my children. We were just about to walk past to get out of the rain, when Hannah and her brother put the brakes on and brought us to a halt. 'What are they doing, Mummy?' asked Hannah. 'Why are they there, Dad?' Then in a loud voice for all to hear, Jonathan said, 'Are they poor?'

Well, Mum and Dad were just about to find a sympathetic and helpful explanation, when Hannah fired more questions: 'What can we do? Can't we have them come and stay with us?' Jonathan added, 'Please can we give them some money?' I have to admit, I wasn't going to stop, but we did. We gave our children a few measly coins and they went over to the rough-looking men, who appeared moved by their gesture.

I learnt a lesson that day: The story of the Good Samaritan haunted the minister who was going to walk by on the other side. Yes, it was reasonable to want to protect Hannah and Jonathan, yet through them God spoke to me. In my children I saw and felt the purity of unconditional love. I was moved by their distress at the reality of homelessness and their surprise at *my* hardness of heart. As I went on to eat my burger and fries, I could hear Jesus saying to me: '. . . *I tell you the truth, whatever you did for one of the least of these brothers of mine, you did for me.' (Matthew 25:40)* Lord, forgive me! In the face of poverty, may *I* never stop asking, 'Why are they there?' That is, until Hannah's question no longer *needs* to be asked.

Bible Readings:

The Good Samaritan	Luke 10:25–37
The greatest commandment	Mark 12:28–34
What does God ask of you?	Deuteronomy 10:12–22

A Prayer

Lord of the friendless,
You spent time with those in need.
You command me to love my neighbour as myself –
regardless of who that may be.
Melt my hardened heart
and give me wisdom to know how I can best serve my sisters
*   and brothers*
in your name. Amen.

49: Cat Lips

Hannah (six years) Jonathan (four years)

If children didn't ask so many questions, then they'd never appreciate how little grown-ups know! Time and time again, my children leave me grappling for answers to their barrage of questions at the meal table. Like the time when Jonathan asked, 'Why don't cats have lips?' Well, I have to say, it wasn't something I'd considered before. I skilfully sidestepped the question leaving it for Frances to field. To her credit, she came up with an imaginative answer: 'As cats lick rather than kiss, perhaps they don't need lips.' Wonderful!

What about another question posed by Hannah: 'Does Jesus like Weetabix?' Where do you start with that one? She also raised the profoundly theological issue: 'How can Jesus be God?' Now we're moving on to puzzles that are not on the minds of children alone.

I'm sure questions should be encouraged. After all, the Bible is full of people seeking answers to difficult questions. From fishermen, to prophets, to kings, and of course, Jesus himself. When I'm wrestling with life's big issues, it's important to be honest and use my mind. However, what do I do when I can't lay my hands on an answer?

I learnt a lesson that day: Perhaps there aren't answers to everything. There'll always be an element of mystery in life. Someone once said, 'An educated person is one who's finally discovered that there are some questions to which nobody has the answer.' Isaac Watts, the hymn writer wrote, *'Where reason fails with all her powers, there faith prevails, and love adores.'* Sometimes, it's trust that's needed.

By the way, if you *do* know why cats don't have lips, there's a small boy and his dad who'd be intrigued to know.

Bible Readings:

A child with a searching mind	Luke 2:41–47
Advice concerning wisdom	Proverbs 3:1–20
His thoughts are not our thoughts	Isaiah 55:6–11

A Prayer

God of Wisdom,
yours is the knowledge that passes all human understanding,
help me to be able to give a reason for the hope I have,
but to be honest about unanswered questions.
May I put my trust in you and not be afraid of mystery,
for the sake of Jesus, my Lord and example. Amen.

The Guest

The pain being over
now I feel the sense of loss.
To see, to touch
caress and kiss
can never be the same
as when my body
was your home.
Then you were mine
and yet not mine.
For when you stirred,
(although that was our secret)
I knew
the life contained within me
was not me.
You were my guest.
My body housed your need
until it grew too great.
And though
a little while
I can sustain you yet,
the first painful
parting's done;
from now
it is all partings.

From me you learn
to walk,
that you can be
the way that
I may learn to tread.

From me you learn
the words,
that you can speak
the truth
that I may comprehend.

From me you suck
the life,
that you can be
the living bread
that I may feed upon
and live.

From me you learn
the love
which is the sword
that pierces my heart through,
and nails you to the cross.

In your necessity
my dearest dear
you were the guest
I entertained.
Now you are host
and at your table
I shall be sustained.

AT SOME TIME OR OTHER!

'The best thing to spend on your children is your time.'

(Anonymous)

50: A Fall Guy

Jonathan (four years)

After yet another scrape on his knee, my son enquired in a weary voice, 'Who keeps on making me fall over? . . . Is it Jesus?'

It was as if he were looking for someone to blame for the inevitable tumbles of an energetic boy, charging around at break-neck speed. I couldn't help but smile at the idea of a divine foot being maliciously placed to trip us up when we're not looking. Yet, however humorous and ludicrous the idea may be, I'm sure Jonathan's not the only person who's blamed God for the downfalls we face in life and the obstacles we frequently confront. In my ministry, I often come across people who have the idea that God is somehow against them and to blame for all their problems; it's as if he's mischievous in some way, waiting to pounce on them!

I learnt a lesson that day: It can be all too easy to point an accusing finger at God and complain about life as though he were somehow putting the boot in! In my heart of hearts, however, I now realise that although there are some things that happen in life that are a frustrating mystery, the underlying truth is that God loves me perfectly and wants the very best for me. That's why he sent Jesus, who wasn't immune from facing trials and tribulations in his own life. God, in his wisdom, may need to allow difficult things to happen, but I don't believe he vindictively sends trouble upon people for no good reason. Rather, he walks with them every step of the way. He's there to help and guide them as they travel their path through life. Like a good mother, or father, he picks up his children when they fall; he embraces them and gives them comfort, encouragement and advice through his Word – the Bible.

Jonathan is bound to face all sorts of tumbles and scrapes throughout his life. It's my hope and prayer that, despite them, he'll discover the depth of his Heavenly Father's love and not blame the One who longs to tend his wounds.

Bible Readings:

Persevere	Romans 5:1–11
Paul faced struggles	Colossians 1:24–2:5
If the Lord had not been on our side	Psalm 124

A Prayer

Gracious God and loving Heavenly Father,
you never promised that life would be easy,
but you have promised to be with me always
and that nothing can separate me from your love in Christ
    Jesus.
May I be assured of this truth in my heart,
share it with others,
and be a channel for your healing Spirit in the world. Amen.

51: As Good as Gold

Hannah (four years)

With her big brown eyes open wide, Hannah often used to
tilt her head to one side and ask Mum or Dad a telling question. This was usually when she was getting ready for bed
and to snuggle down for one last story: 'Have I been good
today?'

The query would be asked with hope if she'd been
naughty and pride if she knew she'd been a good girl. I can
remember on one occasion being totally melted by her
enquiry. In one sense, it didn't matter that she'd pushed the
boundaries a bit too far earlier in the day. At least she was
beginning to grasp the all important art of reflection.
Hannah was starting to realise that her words and actions
(whether good, or not so good) have an impact on others.

I learnt a lesson that day: I decided not to be cross with
Hannah, but to praise her for asking the question and to
answer her honestly, because in that moment, I experienced an overwhelming sense of God's love for me. How
often am I just like Hannah when I pray to my Heavenly
Father? Perhaps I'd do well to be child-like in my reflection:
'Have I, Tony Miles, been good today?'

I believe God knows the answer and is pleased when I
examine my life prayerfully. He is ready to forgive my
shortcomings and Jesus died that I might receive his
pardon and help to change my ways.

Everyone makes mistakes! There are lessons to be learnt
in life and new resolutions to be made in order to live life

according to the Maker's instructions. Moreover, I need to be prepared to forgive those close to me, especially those who've wounded me with a cutting remark or a hurtful action.

Despite my mistakes, I hope that when I eventually fall asleep to this world and reflect on my life's story, my Father God will look upon his child and know my heart. Then I look forward to him telling one last story of my eternal reward in the heavenly places. As for now, with God's help, I want to strive to make each day a good one!

Bible Readings:

The struggle between good and evil	Romans 7:14–25
A wayward son and loving father	Luke 15:11–32
What does the Lord require of you?	Micah 6:1–8

A Prayer

Father, lead me day by day
Ever in thine own good way;
Teach me to be pure and true,
Show me what I ought to do.

John Page Hopps (1834–1911)

52: Remember, Remember . . .

Hannah (seven years) Jonathan (five years)

In preparation for November 5th, my children learnt the 'Sparkler Code' at school. They returned home full of information about fireworks. On bonfire night, Jonathan said, 'Dad, I'm allowed to have sparklers because I'm over five!' That ever-important year made all the difference. Hannah also declared that she needed gloves because 'sparklers are very very hot!'

I learnt a lesson that day: It was all about the importance of *remembering* and the usefulness of 'codes'. The message the school had effectively communicated was: 'Remember the Firework Code.' Of course, learning from the past and paying attention to guidelines is an important discipline for all ages.

Shortly after Guy Fawkes' night is *Remembrance* Sunday, when many reflect upon the pain and suffering caused by past wars in the world. There's a longing that lessons may be learnt and that divided people may be reconciled to each other. Sadly, the sparks of friction still lead to the use of gunpowder or worse, across the nations. Perhaps the longed for peace in the world begins with ordinary people like me, individuals who remember the past and are prepared to work at their own relationships.

So here's my very own *'Peace Code'*, rather than a firework one:

'Remember to follow the teaching of peacemakers, like Jesus. Beware of explosive situations and approach with caution.

Stand well back from unnecessary arguments.
Beware of short fuses and be patient.
Don't put God in your pocket.
Never throw insults around.
Learn how to use 'kid gloves'.
Never cause children to stumble.
And keep pet hates locked up out of harm's way!'

So, why not keep the code throughout the year?
    Peace be with you.

Bible Readings:

Live at peace with everyone	Romans 12:9–21
Love is	1 Corinthians 13:1–13
The beatitudes	Matthew 5:1–12

A Prayer

If only people would live in love and peace with one another;
if only people would heed Jesus' Sermon on the Mount or the
    teaching of St Paul;
then the world would be a different place – a better place!
Merciful Father, forgive.
By your Spirit, turn me into a peacemaker,
    for the kingdom's sake. Amen.

53: Happy Birthday

Jonathan (three years)

Approaching his mum's birthday a few years ago, Jonathan said, '32 is very big, Mummy – like up to the ceiling!' Well, you can understand where he got the idea. From a child's viewpoint it must seem as though you always get taller as you get older. If it's true when you're three, then it must be true when you're thirty-something, or even older. By that reckoning the very elderly Noah would have had his head sticking out of the ark and the oldest man in the Bible, Methuselah, must have been an absolute giant by the time he died at the age of 969!

I learnt a lesson that day: Joking aside, each birthday is an exciting milestone in a child's life, especially when measured on a height chart; whereas adults often want to forget how many times they've heard 'Happy Birthday' sung to them. Yet every year we've been given is a precious gift from God and it may be that *growth* is still important – even if it's not physical!

I'm reminded of the only story we have in the Bible of Jesus as a twelve-year-old boy. Mary and Joseph had lost their son and then found him again a couple of days later in the Temple. We read that: 'Jesus went home and was obedient to them' and he grew in 'wisdom and stature' and 'in favour with God and men'. Perhaps birthdays should be a time when people think about whether they're still growing – not upwards, or even outwards, but inwardly.

So, if it's your birthday today, or in the near future,

perhaps God wants you to consider a 'spiritual check up'. But, don't forget . . . mind your head too!

Bible Readings:

32 is no age!	Genesis 5:21–32
Advice for young and old	Titus 2:1–8
A disastrous birthday banquet!	Mark 6:14–29

A Prayer

Lover of my soul,
may every day,
every hour,
every minute,
every second,
lead me closer to you
and to a deeper experience of you in my life. Amen.

54: St Jonathan?

Jonathan (five years)

It was April 23rd and Jonathan was slumped on the sofa, recovering from a hard day at infant school. Out of the blue he said, 'Did you know that it's St George's Day today, Mummy?' Mum said that she did and ascertained that he'd been learning all about England's patron saint.

St George was a Christian martyr who, in legend, is supposed to have slain a dragon. Very exciting stuff when you're a five-year-old! Jonathan then asked, 'Is there a St Jonathan's Day?' There was a great temptation to reply, 'No way! Not after the way you've behaved today.' Nevertheless, his question was met with a smile.

I learnt a lesson that day: Nobody is *good enough* to be a saint. All of us fall short of our own standards, let alone those God sets for us. Children's misdemeanours are usually fairly obvious and out in the open, whereas adults have learnt to cover up as much as possible. We hide our failings and do our best to appear saintly.

I believe that our Heavenly Father sees right through us and knows what we're really like. You'd have thought that he'd say to us, 'You a saint – no way! Not after the way you've behaved today.' Yet, Christians believe that when we are sorry for our shortcomings and turn to God in honesty, seeking his forgiveness, he clothes us, as it were, with pure white robes. Jesus' death has made a new beginning possible. St John writes: *'If we confess our sins, he is faithful and just and will forgive us our sins and purify us from all unrighteousness.' (1 John 1:9)* What matters is whether we intend in heart and mind to live for God, with his help. In the New Testament 'saints' is the commonest term used to describe Christians. Perhaps *Jonathan's Day* can be when we remember what a saint really is and resolve to slay the dragons within us all!

Bible Readings:

Loved and called to be saints	Romans 1:7–17
Confession and forgiveness	1 John 1:5–10
Living as saints	1 Peter 2:1–12

A Prayer

For all the saints who from their labours rest,
Who thee by faith before the world confessed,
Thy name, O Jesus, be forever blest:
Alleluia, alleluia!

William Walshaw How (1823–1897)

55: Don't Panic!

Hannah (seven years)

School outings are very exciting when you're seven years old. They're much more interesting than sitting in a boring classroom all day. One day, Hannah was due to visit an ancient town, to learn about Roman times. She and her sandwiches needed to be at school by 8.30 am. Well, life in our house is always hectic in the mornings, but this one seemed even more stressful than usual. We only just made it to school in time. A teacher urging Hannah to 'Hurry up' met us at the gate! The pressure was on the staff to register the children and get them ready for departure. Frances was just about to leave the playground when a breathless Hannah came bounding up to her again: 'I've left my lunch behind!' she said in a panic. Mother and daughter immediately started to run out of the school gate, realising that they may well miss the coach.

'But Hannah, you had your rucksack with you. Are you sure you've forgotten it?' said Mum, as she jogged along. Suddenly the two of them stopped and froze for a moment. It dawned on Hannah that she might not have left it behind after all. They turned around and ran back towards Hannah's classroom, passing a stream of children making their way to the coach. Thankfully, I can report that Hannah found her rucksack safely sitting *under her desk*! The bundle was just where she'd left it a few moments before. There was relief all round and she made it onto the coach and enjoyed the outing in glorious weather.

I learnt a lesson that day: When Frances had got her breath back, we laughed about the incident. It made me realise how often I pray to God in despair, desperately asking for help, but without waiting for an answer. If I face a difficult problem today, perhaps I'd do well *not* to panic, but to take a deep breath, pause, pray and then reflect calmly. It may be that I'll discover a clue, or the answer to my prayer, right under my nose – or even under the desk!

Bible Readings:

Jesus' arrest causes panic	Matthew 26:47–56
Three women run away	Mark 16:1–8
Do not fret	Psalm 37:1–9

A Prayer

God of peace,
in the face of the day's challenges,
help me to remain calm and collected.
Teach me to wait patiently and to pray at all times.
I commit my day to you in faith and love,
through Jesus Christ my Lord. Amen.

56: A Shopping List

Hannah (eight years)

It was a Saturday afternoon. Frances was ironing and the children were half watching TV – the tennis at Wimbledon. 'Mum, God answers prayer doesn't he?' said Hannah. Frances nodded encouragingly. 'Well,' she said, 'what if someone asks for a hundred chocolate bars, would God say, 'yes?'' Mum explained that the answer would probably be 'no', because God knows that too much chocolate wouldn't be good for one person and that it would be greedy and selfish too!

Hannah became even more curious: 'Well, what if someone prays for rain to start, and someone else prays for it to stop? What then?' At that point, Frances was wondering where a minister was when you needed one and remembered that I wasn't around. 'That's a very very good question, Hannah, and Mummy doesn't know the answer!'

I learnt a lesson that day: It's a brain baffling mystery *how* God hears all our prayers. The problem of unanswered prayer is tricky! Yet, Jesus did say, *'For everyone who asks receives; he who seeks finds; and to him who knocks, the door will be opened.' (Matthew 7:8)* That doesn't mean we write a shopping list of selfish requests with wishful thinking. Rather, we *ask* for what Jesus would ask for; we *seek* to please God; and we *knock* to find out what is God's perfect will. Unanswered prayer shouldn't necessarily cause me a problem. It may be the answer I didn't realise I was looking for in the first place!

144

But to Hannah I say, 'Tell God what's on your heart. Trust him. Day by day you'll learn what prayer is really all about. Don't be disappointed if God doesn't seem to answer you. Your Heavenly Father always hears you, he knows best and has a reason for everything!'

Bible Readings:

Asking, seeking and knocking	Matthew 7:7–11
Pray at all times	Ephesians 6:18–20
God is near whenever we pray	Deuteronomy 4:5–14

A Reflection

'For I know the plans I have for you', declares the Lord, 'plans to prosper you and not to harm you, plans to give you hope and a future. Then you will call upon me and pray to me, and I will listen to you. You will seek me and find me when you seek me with all your heart.'

Jeremiah 29:11–13

A Child's Prayer

Holy Child, of heavenly birth,
God made manifest on earth,
Fain I would thy follower be,
Live in everything like thee.

Thy humility impart;
Give me thy obedient heart,
Free and cheerful to fulfil
All my heavenly Father's will.

Keep me thus to God resigned,
Till his love delights to find
Fairly copied out on me
All the mind which was in thee.

Charles Wesley (1707–1788)

BACK AT SCHOOL OR THE SHOPS

'What a child is taught on Sunday, he will remember on Monday.'

Welsh Proverb

57: Men Behaving Badly

Jonathan (six years)

Children can stretch their parents' patience to the limit. I'm sure it's not only true in the Miles household. On one occasion, I was getting rather annoyed with my children: to put it bluntly I'd had enough of their squabbling. It was Jonathan who'd pushed things a bit too far. I turned towards him angrily and said in a loud voice for all to hear, 'Jonathan, stop being so childish!' Spontaneously and defiantly he turned to me and replied, 'But Dad, I *am* a child!'

Those passing in the street at that moment, smiled at me sympathetically as I was obviously lost for words. Despite his naughtiness, Jonathan had certainly put me in my place. You see, he was right!

It wasn't long afterwards that I heard about neighbours in Birmingham who'd just settled a 20-year feud over a fir tree! Apparently, they'd taken two decades to stop arguing and get the matter sorted. Well, that kind of behaviour put my children's little tête-à-tête into context.

I learnt a lesson that day: I sadly considered how much time grown-ups spend arguing. Why is it that adults can so easily fall out with each other, family, neighbours or colleagues? Though children need to learn not to argue, young Jonathan was quite right to reprimand me that day. Even though he was misbehaving, at least he did have the excuse of being a child.

In his first letter to the Church at Corinth, St Paul wrote: *'When I was a child, I talked like a child, I thought like a child, I reasoned like a child. When I became a man, I put childish ways behind me.' (1 Corinthians 13:11)*

I'm conscious that if I were to squabble with someone in my son's hearing, it may be cheeky, but he'd have every right to say: 'Stop being childish, Dad!'

Bible Readings:

The disciples argue	Luke 9:46–48
A brother's violent reaction	Genesis 4:1–16
Disagreement amongst leaders	Acts 15:36–41

A Reflection

Love is ... when adults listen to the advice they give to their children and give up their childish ways!

Lord Jesus, help me to be a peacemaker for your kingdom. Amen.

58: Fitting the Bill

Hannah (six years)

Whilst walking home from infant school, Hannah noticed a man riding his bike without a cycle helmet. Mum explained that although it was important to protect our heads, the law didn't require helmets to be worn. Frances went on to reveal that when she was younger seat belts in cars didn't have to be worn either. Yet nowadays, the law says you must wear them. Perhaps one day there'll be a change concerning cycle helmets too. After a few moments, Hannah looked puzzled and said, 'But how *did* Jesus come down and tell people to wear seat belts?' Mum was totally confused, until she realised that our daughter had mis-heard and thought she said, 'the *Lord* says you must wear seat belts.'

Hannah had a really good giggle when she realised her mistake – imagining Jesus as a policeman. Then she asked proudly, 'Would that make a good 'Like A Child' thought for Premier, Dad?' Well, it comes to something when my children are suggesting ideas for radio scripts!

I learnt a lesson that day: As I struggled to write a thought on the theme of 'the *LAW* and the *LORD* in the Bible', my words wouldn't flow properly and to be honest, I was worried because time was against me. Then it dawned on me, perhaps I was trying *too* hard! Surely what was refreshing about that precious moment with Hannah was the fact that she'd learnt to have a good giggle at herself and to tease her dad too!

I believe we need to laugh at our mistakes and ourselves from time to time. Yes, there's a time to be serious, but there's also a time to smile. What's needed is a healthy balance. This isn't *law*, or a saying of our *Lord*; it's simply a pearl of wisdom. So, today's thought: God was the one who gave us a sense of humour, so don't take yourself too seriously!

Bible Readings:

Preachers beware!	Acts 20:7–12
Laugh with Sarah	Genesis 21:1–7
The secret of healthy living	Proverbs 15:30

A Prayer

Creator God,
I thank you for the gift of humour,
for the ability to laugh and smile
and to share a joke with a friend.
When I'm under pressure,
or responsibility weighs heavy,
lighten my spirit and gladden my heart.
May I rejoice in the Lord always
and bring joy to others. Amen.

59: Smart Alec

Hannah (seven years) Jonathan (five years)

It was a Saturday afternoon and I was shopping with the family. My children were getting restless, so they began to look for alternative entertainment. Something more interesting than watching their parents agonise over which shirt would make Dad look trendy on holiday. The next thing I knew was that from inside the shop, Hannah and Jonathan were tapping on the window rather loudly. In the process, they nearly knocked over the finely dressed mannequins on display. Well, that was the last straw. Mum and Dad were getting cross and so we all made a subtle, but sharp exit.

Once outside, Frances and I quickly remonstrated with Hannah and Jonathan about their behaviour. The dialogue went something like this as we addressed our eldest: 'Why were you knocking on the glass, Hannah?' 'Jonathan told me to do it!' she replied innocently. At this her younger brother was just about to protest, when Frances interjected, 'Hannah, if Jonathan told you to jump out of a plane, would you do it?' The answer came as quick as a flash and took us both by surprise: 'Yes, I would, because I'd have a parachute!' It's so difficult being cross when you're laughing. We were impressed at Hannah's quick thinking, which turned our attention from her cheekiness.

I learnt a lesson that day: How often am I full of excuses, rather than standing up to my responsibilities? Sometimes I can be too clever for my own good. I wriggle when I feel guilty before God, rather than being honest with him and following the leading of my conscience. Whilst I may amuse God with my ingenuity and quick thinking, I may be in danger at times of being cheeky or flippant – taking his love and mercy for granted. I may be smart, but the truth is, he will always be smarter. What's more, I'm sure he'll always have the last word, whether it be in this world or the next. Somehow, I don't think God will be impressed if *I* blame *my* younger brother – who happens to be a policeman!

Bible Readings:

The foolishness of God is wiser	1 Corinthians 1:18–2:5
A king tries to cover up his sin	2 Samuel 11
Jesus silences his critics	Mark 2:23–3:6

A Prayer

When I think I'm clever;
when I'm feeling strong and confident;
when I'm boasting with pride;
let your humility wash over me, Lord,
and remind me of the paradoxes of your kingdom;
lest I miss the way of suffering love
and lowly dependence on your grace. Amen.

60: Say it with Flowers

Hannah (six years) Jonathan (four years)

It was the day before Father's Day and Frances was out shopping with our children. 'I have an idea,' said Jonathan, 'let's buy Daddy some flowers.' 'Ermm, well, we don't normally give dads flowers,' said Mum, surprised by Jonathan's suggestion. 'Let's try and find something else!' Hannah thought her brother was just being silly and reprimanded him saying, 'Flowers, Jonathan, are only for mummies!'

Now when I heard about all this, it set me thinking because I don't think anyone has bought me flowers before. What's more, why do I find it slightly embarrassing to admit that I would really have appreciated a gift of carnations?

I learnt a lesson that day: I think we have to beware of certain kinds of social conditioning, especially the sort that says that men and boys should hide their emotions and any appreciation of that which is beautiful. I can remember being greatly moved by the tears that were shed by men and women after the death of the Princess of Wales and by the flowers that were laid in her memory. Saint or no saint, Diana's death was a tragedy which affected a great many people.

10cc may have sung 'Big boys don't cry,' but I think they *do* and should! After all, the shortest verse in the Bible says *'Jesus wept.' (John 11:35)* It was when he lost his close friend Lazarus. He wasn't afraid to show his emotions. He could also appreciate beauty and spoke about flowers.

So, I hope by example I can teach my son to be tough and tender and not be afraid of what others think. It takes a real man to 'Say it with flowers!'

Bible Readings:

Jesus wept	John 11:1–44
Isaiah speaks of flowers	Isaiah 40:6–8
Jesus speaks of flowers	Matthew 6:25–34

A Prayer

For the beauty of the earth,
For the beauty of the skies,
For the love which from our birth
Over and around us lies:

Gracious God, to thee we raise
This our sacrifice of praise.

F. S. Pierpoint (1835–1917) alt.

61: Tears from Heaven

Hannah (seven years)

'The sun shines on the just and the unjust.' Well, if that's true, it must apply to rain as well! Hannah was watching the rain one day with a frown on her little face. She asked: 'When it rains, is it God's tears?' An understandable sentiment and one that I've even heard adults express at wet funerals. Frances and I could see that our daughter was in a thinking mood, so Mum decided to pose a question to Hannah: 'What do you think *would* make God cry?' There was no hesitation, 'If people die, or when they're ill, or if they've been arguing with each other!' It was a very genuine and spontaneous answer, so I resisted the temptation to say, 'No wonder it rains a lot!'

I learnt a lesson that day: I thought about *teardrops from heaven.* What do *I* think causes my Creator pain? Do I make matters worse sometimes? I recall how at the end of Jesus' ministry he came close to Jerusalem and wept over it – knowing it was heading for destruction. I'm sure God must weep today at the state of the wayward world that we live in. He sees and feels all the heartbreak, suffering and pain caused by selfishness, pride and greed. I believe the world has fallen from what God intended it to be.

Although Hannah wasn't literally correct, rain is now for me a reminder of God's deep love for a broken and fragile world. What's more, the rainbow gives me hope of sunshine after the rain. In the storms of life, I hold on to the fact that my faithful Creator will one day wipe away all tears.

Misery and injustice will be replaced with joy and peace for all who trust in his eternal love. So, if Hannah asks me: 'Where *are* God's tears then?' I think I'd have to answer: 'Not far from our own!'

Bible Readings:

Jesus enters Jerusalem and weeps   Luke 19:28–44
The fall   Genesis 3
The flood and the rainbow   Genesis 6:1–9:17

A Prayer

O joy that seekest me through pain,
I cannot close my heart to thee:
I trace the rainbow through the rain,
And feel the promise is not vain,
That morn shall tearless be.

George Matheson (1842–1906)

God of compassion, may I never be ashamed of holy tears.
 Amen.

62: Well Done!

Hannah (seven years) Jonathan (five years)

At the end of a day at infant school, my children would stroll across the playground looking very tired. Nevertheless, they often had a broad grin on their faces, making it clear they were itching to tell you something. It didn't take long before they were showing off their achievement stickers. The school always positively encouraged children to help them feel they were making progress and doing well. Frequently Hannah and Jonathan emerged proudly with messages on their jumpers, such as: 'I'm a good reader!', or 'Maths wizard', or 'Super Speller'. I think I missed out somehow when I was at school.

On one occasion when counting all his stickers, Jonathan even asked his mum whether his teacher could baby-sit one day, so that she could see his fine sticker collection that he'd stuck all over his wardrobe!

I learnt a lesson that day: Everyone needs encouragement – like the flower bud needs the warm sun to help it blossom! Most people feel a little insecure at times and lack the confidence they need to achieve their full potential. I believe that God, through the warmth of his love and mercy, wants to help us to grow and bloom. Through the light of his Son, Jesus, he gently draws people to himself. He longs to forgive those who fail, lift the fallen, strengthen the weak, set people free in spirit and nurture them on their journey through life. God also calls his children to help each other and to be a community of encouragement.

So, who can I encourage or praise today? I may not get a sticker but, in humility, may I hear the gentle whisper of God affirming me: *'Well done, good and faithful servant!'* *(Matthew 25:23 and 26)*

Bible Readings:

Paul's encouragement to a church	Ephesians 1:15–23
Moses ensures Joshua is encouraged	Deuteronomy 1:26–40
Good and faithful servant	Matthew 25:14–30

A Prayer

Lord Jesus,
your servant Barnabas was called 'Son of Encouragement'.
I read in Acts of the Apostles that he was a good man
full of the Holy Spirit and faith;
that he urged people to be faithful
and true to the Lord with all their hearts.
Grant me the encouragement I need
and help me to bear the qualities of Barnabas
as I come alongside other people,
for the sake of your kingdom. Amen.

63: What's in a Name?

Hannah (seven years) Jonathan (five years)

As they strolled home from school, my children were chatting away about their Christian names. They seemed happy with them – which is just as well! I think it's a shame when children dislike what they're called. I always feel sorry for the son of Mr and Mrs Sprout who'd been given the name *Russell*. Hardly fair!

Frances and I explained to our children that we chose their names very carefully. Nevertheless, they both wondered what God thought about them. Did *he* like what they were called? It was at this point that Hannah said, 'Wouldn't it be funny if there was another family in the world with the names Tony, Frances, Hannah and Jonathan.' 'Could there be another?' Mum asked herself. After a while Jonathan giggled, 'Cor, there definitely wouldn't be a family with the same middle names *and* first names! I guess he's right. The odds would be even worse than winning the National Lottery – not that I'd know much about that!

I learnt a lesson that day: As it dawned on my children that they were special, not only to Mum and Dad, but also to God, I was reminded of a lovely verse in the Bible where God says to his people: *'Fear not, for I have redeemed you; I have summoned you by name; you are mine.' (Isaiah 43:1b)* He goes on to say that they are precious in *his* sight, honoured and loved by him.

So, it doesn't matter how many Hannahs and Jonathans

there are in the world, they're all individually *precious*. I find that comforting, but also challenging. For surely, all crowds are gatherings of individuals who are loved by their Creator. So, each person is worthy of my respect and care. Therefore, I shouldn't lump people together into impersonal groups like the 'homeless', the 'disabled', the 'starving' or even the 'enemy'. I need to pray for them as individuals who are loved by God. To care in this way may mean that I, Tony, am being called by name to stand out from the crowd!

Bible Readings:

God calls his people by name	Isaiah 43:1–13
A special boy is named	Luke 1:57–66
From slave to son	Philemon 1–25

A Reflection

I am loved more than I could ever imagine.
I am known by name and I am unique.
There will never be another me
and I'm valued for who I am.
I am a precious useful child of God,
with a future in his care.
I am to love,
because Jesus first loved me.

The Love of a Child

When a child is born,
everyone is filled
with emotion and wonder
at the beauty of the babe.

There is nothing,
in this world today,
more wonderful than
the love of a child.

A child's love is something
so very precious.
It works more miracles
than we ever imagined.

To receive this love
and to return it
is the greatest of
all God's gifts.

From 'Fleeting Thoughts' by Mollie Elborough.
© 1998 Miles Publishing House.
Used with kind permission.

Mollie Elborough is Grandmother to Tony
and Great Grandmother to Hannah and Jonathan.

BACK AT HOME

'You know that God knows whatever I'm going to do next . . . well, I want to surprise him so he doesn't know!'

Hannah Miles (seven years)

64: Two Things at Once

Hannah (five years)

Someone once said, 'The only thing that children wear out faster than shoes are parents and teachers!' Well, on one occasion, my children were in a particularly wearing mood. They were relentlessly asking their mum for this and that and she was getting harassed. She didn't have time to think for herself, let alone get on with what she was doing. She was just about to explode when I returned home, intervening with the coolness and calmness of a bomb disposal expert.

I explained firmly that as much as she'd like to, a mummy couldn't do more than one thing at a time. As quick as a flash, Hannah replied indignantly, 'Oh yes she can, she's got two hands, hasn't she?' Well, sometimes the logic of a small child can certainly melt an angry moment and bring about a smile.

I learnt a lesson that day: Although children can't have what they want all the time, perhaps I should remember that from their point of view, the housework, and 101 other things that occupy parents, aren't as important as spending time with them.

Time is precious and children grow up all too quickly. If I don't find enough time for them, one day I may find they'll be too busy for me! It's hard to juggle priorities, but do I create sufficient space for those I love? Do I reserve enough time for my children, parents, friends and neighbours? What about the stranger in the midst, too?

It would seem that Jesus used the *'two hands'* God had given him. Even though he was a busy man, with the whole world to save, he managed to find time for people.

Bible Readings:

Jesus makes time for children	Matthew 19:13–15
Jesus makes time for Zacchaeus	Luke 19:1–10
Entertaining strangers	Hebrews 13:1–3

A Prayer

Almighty God and patient loving Father,
the fact that you always have time for me
is a mystery I cannot fully understand.
Though it will mean making sacrifices,
help me to give people my time and attention.
May I never be too busy to care
and grant me wisdom to keep my life in balance,
for Jesus' sake. Amen.

65: Jump for Jesus!

Hannah (four years)

A young child who's getting to grips with Sunday school is a challenge for any parent. A little knowledge naturally leads on to a whole host of taxing questions that need answers now, not tomorrow. On one occasion my wife was explaining to our daughter that Christians believe in a risen Jesus who lives inside us – if we love him. This kindled Hannah's imagination as she listened to Mum's words of faith and wisdom. Then came a reply from this little girl who's prone to using an old bed as a trampoline: 'But if Jesus lives inside me and I jump up and down, does that mean he'll fall out?'

I'll never forget that one. It was very tempting to say, 'Not if you keep your mouth shut!' but that would be unfair! In fact, from a four-year-old, it was a very good question.

I learnt a lesson that day: I believe that Jesus does dwell within the Christian. The Bible says believers should be continually filled with the Spirit. Hannah made me ask myself a simple question: 'Can Jesus *fall out* of me?'

It then dawned on me that in any human relationship, we can fall in and out of love. Likewise, if Christians are not careful, their love for Jesus can become lukewarm too, or even cold. Nothing will stop him loving them, but if they forget him, or stop communicating with him or think only of themselves, then they may find that Jesus is squeezed out of their lives.

So, I need to nurture my relationship with the Lord. If I do, one thing's for sure, he'll never leave me or forsake me. After all, he wants to be in my heart, through all the ups and downs of life!

Bible Readings:

Warning for a lukewarm Church	Revelation 3:14–22
Moses encourages Joshua	Deuteronomy 31:1–8
Be careful how you live	Ephesians 5:1–20

A Prayer

Lord Jesus,
thank you for knocking on the door of my heart.
You are a welcome guest and I invite you to dwell within me.
Possess every part of me with your love
and fill me with your Holy Spirit.
May I never become lukewarm or distant in my relationship
*   with you;*
rather may I be strong and courageous
in the knowledge that you have promised to be with me
wherever my faith journey takes me.
For your kingdom's sake. Amen.

66: A Painful Spell

Jonathan (six years)

It was one of those difficult moments when as a parent you're not sure what to do for the best. Jonathan had just shut two of his fingers in a door by accident. He was understandably screaming and crying. Mum immediately put his hand under a tap of running cold water and swept him into her arms to cuddle him. That's all he wanted – so he didn't let go! After a while, he managed to fight back the tears and said with a curled bottom lip: 'Mum, how do you spell "ow?"'

Spelling is one of Jonathan's strong points and he desperately wanted to know how to express his feelings in words. Mum wasn't quite sure, but as they talked it seemed to take his mind off his throbbing fingers.

I learnt a lesson that day: I don't always find it easy to articulate or express my feelings – let alone spell out how I feel in detail. For example: consider some of the dreadful things that happen in this country and on the rest of the planet too; the cruelty, suffering, murder and intolerance. I often groan and weep inside as I listen to the news. What can you say? How terribly difficult it must be to pray if you are one of the innocent victims of evil in the world. In the Bible, St Paul talks about the world groaning in pain, but the Spirit of God helps us in our weakness. He says: *'We do not know what we ought to pray for, but the Spirit himself intercedes for us with groans that words cannot express.' (Romans 8:26)*

Perhaps all I need to do is come alongside people in their pain and brokenness; to weep and ache with care for them and allow the Spirit of God to pray through me and minister to those in need. With faith, I trust that God will enfold them with his everlasting arms that will never let them go. Thanks be to God, that we don't need to be able to spell everything out, because *he* knows and weeps with us!

Bible Readings:

Groans that words cannot express	Romans 8:18–27
David pours out his heart	Psalm 142
God of all comfort	2 Corinthians 1:3–11

A Prayer

All-Knowing and Ever-Present Father,
when I run out of words
or the pain is too great,
may I rest securely in your love
and let your Spirit of comfort and healing flow through me.
Then, with patience and endurance,
may I find the strength to come alongside others,
upheld by the One who is interceding for me. Amen.

67: Daring to be Different

Jonathan (five years)

Jonathan was standing in front of the mirror brushing his hair before school. It was quite funny watching a young boy admiring his reflection. Then, all of a sudden, he said: 'Mummy, when is my hair going to die?' It seemed a strange question, but Mum had a go at answering off the top of her head – if you can excuse the pun! 'Well, it's not really going to die as such,' she said, 'hair keeps on growing.' I half expected Jonathan to bring up my bald patch, but thankfully he didn't. There was just a silence. So, Frances asked him the reason for his question: 'Because I want to have my hair dyed like Martin's!' Everything then quickly fell into place. Martin was a teenager known to Jonathan who'd recently had his hair bleached. The English language can be so very confusing to a young child.

I learnt a lesson that day: It was amazing to think that at our son's tender age he was already beginning to consider his image. Sadly, it's cool to believe the phrase 'image is everything'. It's human nature to want to fit in with the crowd and to copy those we look up to. Fashions, like bleached hair, may be quite harmless, but there are other subtle trends that are more of a concern to me as a Christian parent. Image may be important, yet it isn't always healthy and certainly isn't everything.

I believe God is concerned about what I'm like on the inside. He wants me to have the strength of character to become a holy trendsetter, rather than simply a follower of others. Jesus dared to be different and didn't conform to the expectations of those around him, especially the religious leaders of his day. Rather he showed us an alternative way and *died* so that we might all be born again to a radical new lifestyle – one that's inside out! I hope one day Jonathan will aspire to being radical like that.

Bible Readings:

The Lord looks at the heart	1 Samuel 16:1–13
Messiah won't judge by sight	Isaiah 11:1–9
Do not conform any longer	Romans 12:1–8

A Prayer

Lord Jesus,
you didn't conform to other people's expectations,
rather, you went against the flow
and remained true to your calling.
Help me to have the courage of my convictions
and to be original and authentic.
I thank you that you didn't judge people by appearances,
but that you were only concerned about the heart.
That's cool with me.
Help me to go and do likewise. Amen.

68: Tricycle Theology

Jonathan (four years)

Cynically, someone once said, 'People see more of God in the garden than they do in the Church.' A sweeping statement, but possibly true for Jonathan. One day he was happily riding his little tricycle around the garden when suddenly he called out at the top of his voice, 'Mum, I want to ask you something.' Well, Frances left the kitchen to join him in the sunshine. 'What is it?' she said. There was the inevitable pause and a deep breath, followed by, 'Is Jesus really God?' There was another pause whilst Frances tried to think how on earth she was going to explain the mystery of the incarnation to a four-year-old and the fact that Jesus was human, yet Divine too! She made do with a simple, 'Yes he is!' 'Oh,' said Jonathan, 'I hadn't thought of that before.' Then off he rode on his bike again – as happy as Larry!

Three days later, on the way to play school, Jonathan said to his friend Christopher: 'Do you know that Jesus is really God?' Christopher was really impressed and Frances and I were proud of our little evangelist!

I learnt a lesson that day: Children are naturally inquisitive, trusting and keen to share what they know. These are three qualities that I could do with nurturing myself. It's so easy for Christians to keep quiet about the significance of Jesus because we don't know the answers to all the knotty questions. There will always be an element of mystery, but that shouldn't put me off. For people might see more of

God in the Church if Christians like me were more willing to get on their bikes and share what they've learnt about Jesus through their words and deeds.

Bible Readings:

Philip shares his faith	Acts 8:26–40
Jesus sends out the 72	Luke 10:1–20
Daniel stands up for his faith	Daniel 6

A Reflection

Let earth and heaven combine,
Angels and men agree,
To praise in songs divine
The incarnate Deity,
Our God contracted to a span,
Incomprehensibly made man.

Charles Wesley (1707–1788)

There's so much I don't understand, Lord,
but let me be content to share what I know to be true in my
*   heart. Amen.*

69: Show Me the Way to Go Home

Jonathan (five years) Callum (five years) – Jonathan's friend

Jonathan had a friend to tea after his day at infant school. They'd had a great time together and afterwards Frances offered to take the young boy home. It wasn't until they'd begun the car journey that Frances realised she wasn't sure of where he lived. 'Do you know the way, Callum?' she said. The little boy shook his head. 'Oh dear,' said Frances. 'Well, what's the name of the street, or your house number?' 'I don't know!' he said seriously, 'But I can *show* you the way!'

Frances had a rough idea where she had to go, but Callum needed to give his directions using words and gestures. They had great fun and soon arrived at the right road. Eventually, there was a triumphant cheer from the back seat, 'There it is! It's the one with the red car outside.'

A five-year-old couldn't answer all the technical questions, but he'd learnt the way to go. What's more, he could recognise the final destination. It was a good job the car was there.

I learnt a lesson that day: To follow Jesus is to begin a journey. The longer I travel his way, the more I understand the journey and can make sense of it. Gradually, the finer details gradually fit into place and I become more mature. It's then I feel I can begin to give a reason for the faith that's in me.

Sometimes people ask deep questions about Christianity, yet I've learnt that I shouldn't worry if I can't put my answers into words. All I have to do is point people in the right direction or show them the way – hopefully taking them with me! I shouldn't feel inadequate, but simply trust what I know to be true in my heart and keep my eyes on Jesus. The wonderful thing is he's always there if I seek him. So I too can let out a triumphant cheer: 'Here he is – the Way, the Truth and the Life!'

Bible Readings:

Seek with all your heart	Jeremiah 29:11–14
Seek and you will find	Luke 11:9–10
Jesus the way to the Father	John 14:1–14

A Prayer

Guide me, O Lord my God,
for you have promised that I will find you if I seek you with all
*   my heart.*
Help me to follow the way of Jesus,
to believe in his truth
and receive the gift of eternal life.
Grant me the confidence to point others in the same direction,
for the sake of Christ, my Lord and Saviour. Amen.

70: PC, or Not PC? – That is the Question!

Hannah (seven years) Jonathan (five years)

It was early one Saturday evening and the Miles family was watching television. We were enjoying a talented singer who was performing a very catchy song, when Jonathan said, 'Look, she's fat!' Next, without taking her eyes off the screen, his sister Hannah said, 'No, you should say she's *big looking*!' Frances and I smiled, impressed by Hannah's attempt to be politically correct. We then pointed out that the singer may be on the large side, but she was also very pretty. As quick as a flash Jonathan replied, 'Pretty fat you mean!' I confess I laughed. I couldn't help it. It was very funny coming from someone so young. Little children say what they think and can't help commenting on what they see – usually quite innocently but loudly and often in the presence of the person concerned. Rather like the time when Jonathan said, 'Mummy, why are you looking nice today?' Whoops, he'll have to do better than that when he gets his first girlfriend.

I learnt a lesson that day: Jonathan will have to learn the art of diplomacy and how to hold his tongue occasionally, rather than saying things that could be hurtful. Yet, notwithstanding that, it's refreshing to hear the pure uncomplicated honesty of children. Adults may grow in sensitivity, but there's a real danger that we become so sensitive that we never say anything about anything.

I think Jesus got the balance right. He chose his words carefully and was loving and wise. However, he also knew when to speak out like a child – often with the words: 'I tell you the truth.' I'm reminded of a verse from the Old Testament: there's '. . . *a time to be silent and a time to speak, . . .' (Ecclesiastes 3:7b)* There's also a time to finish, like now!

Bible Readings:

A time for everything	Ecclesiastes 3:1–8
Taming the tongue	James 3:1–12
Jesus writes on the ground	John 7:53–8:11

A Prayer

Tongues are funny things to look at, Lord.
Who'd have thought that such a peculiar part of my anatomy
could be so powerful.
Your servant James likened it to a fire –
it can rage uncontrolled and render religion worthless;
my tongue can curse or bless!
Jesus, I want you to be Master of all of me,
including my tongue.
By your Spirit grant me self control
and wisdom in all I do today,
that I may know when to speak
and when to draw circles in the sand quietly. Amen.

Childhood

Thank you, Lord, for making me so small.
I enjoyed the large room
and all the large people.
But why, Lord, when I spoke to them
did they smile and speak to each other?
Why were their words, their cups, their saucers,
their sips, their laughs and their voices, bigger than mine?
I spoke of football; so they spoke of Bach.
I talked of schooldays; so they mentioned wine.
I longed to be loved; so they patted the sofa, and then the dog.
All I suggested, they countered;
all I tried, they loved to ignore.
Lord, I have lived only in days, but they in years.
I know so little, they know so much.
But unlike them,
I can eat more little cakes without getting fat,
I can climb more stairs without getting puffed.
I can sleep more soundly than they who need pills.
Perhaps, Lord, one day I shall be like them, but I pray not.
Meanwhile, I am most thankful good Lord,
for your making me so small, else how could I see
what is really in this large room,
with all these large people
who are really – quite small.

Hosea 11:1–11 – God's Love for Israel

[1] 'When Israel was a child, I
  loved him,
and out of Egypt I called my son.
[2] But the more I called Israel,
the further they went from me.
They sacrificed to the Baals
and they burned incense to
  images.
[3] It was I who taught Ephraim to
  walk,
taking them by the arms;
but they did not realise
it was I who healed them.
[4] I led them with cords of human
  kindness,
with ties of love;
I lifted the yoke from their neck
and bent down to feed them.

[5] Will they not return to Egypt
and will not Assyria rule over
  them
because they refuse to repent?
[6] Swords will flash in their cities,
will destroy the bars of their
  gates
and put an end to their plans.
[7] My people are determined to
  turn from me.
Even if they call to the Most
  High,
he will by no means exalt them.

[8] How can I give you up,
  Ephraim?
How can I hand you over, Israel?
How can I treat you like
  Admah?
How can I make you like
  Zeboiim?
My heart is changed within me;
all my compassion is aroused.
[9] I will not carry out my fierce
  anger,
nor will I turn and devastate
  Ephraim.
For I am God, and not man –
the Holy One among you.
I will not come in wrath.
[10] They will follow the LORD;
he will roar like a lion.
When he roars,
his children will come trembling
  from the west.
[11] They will come trembling
like birds from Egypt,
like doves from Assyria.
I will settle them in their homes,'
declares the LORD.

Thanksgiving: New Song

Suggested tune: 'Normandy' 8.7.8.7.D (C. Bost 1790–1874)

Lord, to you, we sing a new song;
age old faith has seen us through.
As we gather now to worship,
let our minds explore anew –
Father, Son and Holy Spirit,
this our God, the three in one.
What a myst'ry! What a wonder!
Blessed truth to us has come.

So, to God, as heav'nly Father,
thanks and praise we offer you.
By your Word you have created,
given life, sustained it too.
Through the good times, and the bad
times,
never has your love grown cold.
Help us see your plan and purpose,
God of mercy, heal the world.

And, to God, in Saviour, Jesus,
thanks and praise we offer you.
Born on earth, you dwelt among us,
showed us, taught us, loved by few.
We rejected, crucified you,
on the cross you died in pain.
O forgive us! Grant your promise,
let us share new life again.

Now, to God, eternal Spirit,
thanks and praise we offer you.
Breath of Life, come breathe upon
us,
lead us in the work we do.
Make us people who are holy,
help us bear your fruit of love.
Take us, break us, and remake us,
Come, descend now, like a dove.

Praise the Lord now, from the
heavens,
praise Him from the heights above,
praise Him all His glorious angels,
praise with us the God of love.
He is worthy of our worship,
lift our hearts to let Him reign.
All the world, yes all creation,
raise and magnify His Name!

About NCH

NCH is one of the UK's leading children's charities, running over 480 projects and working with 98,000 children, young people and their families. It is also the children's charity of the Methodist Church. Our intention of *'Helping the children who need it the most'* reflects John Wesley's words: 'Go not only to those who need you but to those who need you the most.'

We are ambitious for children and believe that all children and young people should have the support and opportunities to reach their full potential, no matter how difficult their circumstances and need. Through our wide range of projects we make a real difference to the lives of children, young people and their families. We develop and run services in response to local need and campaign for change in partnership with our service users.

NCH was founded in 1869 as The Children's Home by a Methodist minister, Rev. Dr Thomas Bowman Stephenson. This was both a personal response and later one made on behalf of the church, to rescue destitute children from extreme poverty and the danger of living on the streets. The Home was a radical step in the days when the poor and destitute could expect to end up in the workhouse. Stephenson did not set out to found orphanages or institutions. Instead the Homes reflected his far-sighted commitment to a family-based model of care with half a dozen children in the care of a housemother and housefather.

The pioneering vision of Stephenson continued to be important in the growth of the organisation. NCH was the first organisation to develop professional training for those looking after children during the 1880s. We campaigned for the legal recognition of adoption and became one of the first registered adoption agencies in 1926. In 1935, NCH published a *Children's Charter* that predates the United Nations Declaration of the Rights of the Child.

In the 1960s the work of the National Children's Home saw a shift towards more preventative action, working to support vulnerable parents in their communities and that community-based work has continued to the present day.

Today, our work draws on over 130 years of experience of finding solutions to the problems faced by children and young people. The values and principles that motivated Stephenson still underpin our continuing commitment to help vulnerable children and young people realise their individual, unique potential.

The partnership between the Methodist Church and NCH remains as strong as ever, with the shared vision of a just society at the heart of the relationship. Without the loyal support of the Methodist Church, we could not continue to help the children who need it the most.

Rev. Bill Lynn, Pastoral Director, NCH

The NCH Covenant

Every child has the right to live, to be safe and to be loved. Every young person has the right to be housed, to have enough money to live in dignity and to have enough support for the future. Every young person has the right to justice, to realise their potential and to be given the space to become independent. In an often cruel and imperfect world, we uphold the work of NCH with children and young people in danger, in need and at risk. We support the growth of this work and the pursuit of all these rights for the young, the discounted and the vulnerable. We make this covenant with NCH for the sake of all God's children.

Amen

The second Sunday in July is designated by the Methodist Church as NCH Sunday to celebrate the work of the charity and the anniversary of the opening of the first home.

www.nch.org.uk

Supporter Helpline   0845 7 626579

Registered charity no. 215301

Scripture Index

Unless marked in *italics*, references are Thoughts not pages.

184

General Index

Very common subjects are not listed as they appear frequently: e.g. Father, Jesus, Sprit, Holy Spirit, kingdom of God, child, Mum, Dad, Hannah and Jonathan etc.

187

188

189

191